UNDER THE DRAGON FLAG

SR Scholarly Resources Inc.
Wilmington, Delaware · London

SCHOLARLY RESOURCES, INC.
Wilmington, Delaware • London

Reprint edition published in 1973
First published in 1898 by William Heinemann,
    London

Reprinted from an original in the
University of Michigan Library

Library of Congress Catalog Card Number: 72-82087
ISBN: 0-8420-1383-0

Manufactured in the United States of America

UNDER
THE DRAGON FLAG

My Experiences in the Chino-Japanese War

BY

JAMES ALLAN

LONDON
WILLIAM HEINEMANN
1898

UNDER THE DRAGON FLAG

CHAPTER I

THE following narrative is a record of my experiences during the late memorable war between China and Japan. Without going into any detailed account of my earlier life, some few facts concerning myself are probably necessary for the better understanding of the circumstances which led up to the events here presented. It will be obvious that I can make no claim to literary skill; I have simply written down my exact and unadorned remembrance of incidents which I witnessed and took part in. Now it is all over I wonder more and more at the slightness of the hazard which suddenly placed me at such a period in so strange an experience.

I am the son of a Lancashire gentleman who accumulated considerable wealth in the cotton trade. He died when I was still a boy. I found myself, when I came of age, the possessor of upwards of £80,000. Thus I started in life as a man of fortune ; but it is due to myself to say that I took prompt and effectual measures to clear myself of that invidious character. Not to mince matters needlessly, I ran through that eighty thousand pounds in something short of four years. I was not in the least "horsey" ; my sphere was the gaieties of Paris and the gaming-tables of Monte Carlo—a sphere which has made short work of fortunes compared with which mine would be insignificant. The pace was fast and furious ; I threw out my ballast liberally as I went along, and the harpies, male and female, who surrounded me, picked it up. Bright and fair enough was the prospect as I started on the road to ruin ; gloomy the clouds that settled round me as I approached that dismal terminus. Then, when too late, I began to regret my folly. I seemed to wake as if from a dream, from a state of helpless infatuation, in which my acts were scarcely the effect of my own volition. The general out-look became decidedly uninviting.

About eleven o'clock one spring night of the year 1892, I was standing close to the railings of the Whitworth Park in my native city of Manchester, to whose dull provincial shades I had retired at the enforced close of my creditable career. I remember that I was engaged in wondering what on earth I could have done with all my money, the only tangible return for which appeared to be an intimate and peculiar knowledge of the French language and of certain undesirable phases of French life. The hour, as I have said, was late, and Moss Lane, the street in which I stood disconsolate, dark and deserted. Presently there came along towards me a man whose uncertain gait was strongly suggestive of the influence of alcohol. He stopped upon reaching me, and asked if I could direct him to Victoria Park. This is an extensive semi-private enclosure, where numbers of the plutocracy of Cottonopolis have their residences. One of its several gates is nearly opposite the spot where Moss Lane leads into Oxford Street, which fact I communicated to my questioner. To my surprise he, by way of acknowledgment, struck his hand into mine and shook it fervently.

" Shake hands, shake hands," he said ; " that's right—you're talking to a gentleman, though you mightn't think it."

I certainly should not have thought it. He was a short, thick-set man, of about five feet and two or three inches, shabbily dressed ; and his unsteady lurch, swollen features, and odorous breath, told plainly of a heavy debauch. Amused by his manner,

I entered into conversation with him. He was, it appeared, a sailor, a Lancashire man, and, if he was to be believed, very respectably connected in Manchester. I gathered that he had ended a boyhood of contumacy by running away to sea, his people, though they had practically disowned him, allowing him a pound a week. This allowance had for some time past been stopped, and he was coming up in person to investigate the why and wherefore. Having a week or two before come off a voyage at Liverpool, he had at that port drawn £75 in pay, which he had spent in two days and nights of revelry, an assertion to which his personal appearance bore strong corroborative testimony. He appeared, on the whole, to consider himself an exceedingly ill-used person. " I'm a houtcast," he repeatedly said. I asked him in what capacity he served on shipboard. "A.B.," he replied, " always A.B.;" and certainly, in speech and appearance, he seemed nothing better than a foremast man, although, shaking hands with me again and again, he each time asseverated that it was the hand of a gentleman. At length he went on his way, and I stood watching his receding figure as he reeled down the street. I was just turning away, when I heard a loud outcry ; the "houtcast," about a hundred yards distant, was hailing me. On what trifles does destiny depend !

My first impulse was to walk off without taking
any notice of his shouts, and on the simple decision
to stay and see what he wanted, turned the whole
future. It appeared that whilst talking with me
his obfuscated mind had lost the directions I had
given him as to the locality of Victoria Park.
Having nothing in particular to do, I volunteered
to walk along with him, and keep him in the right
direction, and accordingly we entered the park
together. With considerable difficulty, he found
out the road and house he was in search of; I
doubt if, without my aid, he would have found it
at all in his then condition. He had not, he
informed me, been in Manchester for years, and
those he was looking up had changed their residence.
The exterior of the place, when found, seemed to
bear out his statement as to the social position of
his relatives. I asked him what sort of reception
he thought he would get from them.

"He did not," he replied, "care a d——n
what it might be, but he was going to see why
they had stopped his quid, and no mistake about
it."

He extended to me an invitation to come in with
him "and have a drink," a courtesy which, needless
to say, I declined. He then left me, after another
vehement handshaking, and proceeded up the drive
in front of the house. A feeling of curiosity to see

what kind of greeting the drunken, wastrel "hout-cast" would command from his folk, all uncon-scious of his disagreeable proximity to their emi-nently respectable residence, induced me to follow him.   I paused at a point where, concealed by some shrubbery, I had a view of the hall door, which, upon my friend's ringing, was opened by a smart maid-servant. Swaying up and down on the steps in a most ludicrous manner, the "hout-cast" addressed her, although I was too far off to make out the words, but to judge by her looks she felt no prepossession in his favour.   After a while she went away, leaving the door open and him standing on the steps.   In about a minute a stout, middle-aged gentleman appeared from the brightly-lighted hall, his whole aspect presenting the strongest possible contrast to that of the seedy mariner.   The conference between them was brief and angry, and terminated with the gentleman's returning within and slamming the door in the other's face, who, with his hands in his pockets, stood for some time planted where he was, staring at the *visage de bois* as if dumfounded.   Then he applied himself vigorously to the bell, and pulled with might and main.   This course of treatment having no effect, he commenced shouting a series of objurgations much too vigorous to be here set down. No response, of course, was forthcoming, and at length the discomfited visitor turned slowly away from the inhospitable mansion. I rejoined him as he staggered past me. He showed no surprise at seeing me again, but contented himself with simply asking me where the —— I had been. From what he said in answer to my questions, it appeared that they had had the brutality to tell him to call when he was sober,—" as if," said he, with a good many curses, " I wasn't sober enough for them. Wouldn't even give me a night's shelter. But it's always how they've treated me—a houtcast, that's what I am—a houtcast."

Apparently hard hit, the "houtcast," who for the time being certainly had some grounds for so styling himself, leaned with his back against the gate, as if the effort to stand upright was too much for him on the top of his recent disappointment. His plight was undoubtedly pitiable. He had no money, it was well after midnight, the city was distant, and moreover the search for a lodging would in his condition be a matter of time and difficulty. Taking pity on his forlorn state, I offered him the shelter of my own roof for the night, an offer he was not slow to accept, remarking that one gentleman should help another ; and that if I had any " tidy brandy " he would be able to get on well enough until to-morrow. So we set out for my lodgings in Cecil Street.

This chance meeting was the beginning of a long
and intimate acquaintance.   In the course of conversation I disclosed to Charles Webster—such
was his name—the desperate state of my affairs,
with the gloomy prospect they entailed.   The
remedy he proposed—and when sober he spoke
well and sensibly—was drastic and by no means
unfeasible.   "Cut it all and go to sea," he said.
" You've enjoyed yourself while your money lasted,
and what's the good of money but to spend?
You've spent yours—now go to sea and get some
more.   That's how I do—have a regular good
blow-out when I draw my pay, and then ship for
another voyage."

"That is all very well for you," I replied, "but
how can I, without either training or experience,
get a berth on board ship ? "

" I can do it for you," replied Webster.   "Lots
of vessels are ordered to sea in a hurry, and not
particular in picking up a crew, or perhaps a trifle
over-loaded or not properly found, and short-
handed in consequence.   That's the sort of craft
I'd look out for you, and if one wouldn't take you,
another would.   I'd tog you out like an A.B., and
swear you knew your duty."

"And what when they found I didn't ? "

" Wouldn't matter a straw when we were afloat.
All they could do would be to d——n my eyes or

yours and make the best of it. It's done every day.
Certificates go for nothing, they're so easily obtained.
When the voyage was over, you'd be up to a thing
or two, and the skipper would rather sign your
papers than be at the bother of going and swearing
you weren't a thorough seaman ; then you could
get another job without me. It's done constantly,
I tell you, and why not ? Nobody can do anything without learning. You take a trip with
me, and I'll make a sailor of you. You've stood
by me like a gentleman, and I'll give you a lift if
I can."

Well, to cut the story short, I resolved, after
some cogitation, to follow his advice, as, in the circumstances to which I had contrived to reduce
myself, I saw nothing better to do. My introduc-
tion to a seafaring life was effected pretty much
on the lines indicated in the foregoing conversation.
The change from the existence of a voluptuary,
squandering thousands on the wanton pleasure of
the moment, to that of a common sailor, was at
first anything but agreeable, and often and bitterly
did I curse the follies of the past. However, we
learn from experience, and probably I have profited
by the unpalatable lesson. Webster was a firm
ally, and showed that despite his dissolute and
reckless mode of living, he really did possess something of the character which he claimed, that of a

gentleman. Under his tuition, and being moreover,
like Cuddie Headrigg, "gleg at the uptak," I made
rapid progress in knowledge.

We made several voyages together. In the
summer of the year 1894 we were in San Francisco,
and rather at a loose end ; Webster with a good
deal of money in his possession, and spending it as
usual in riotous living. We were intimate at this
time with a man named Francis Chubb, an Aus-
tralian by birth, an able seaman, and a very reckless, daring, and resolute character. To him it is
owing that I have this tale to tell. One night as
we were sitting over our potations, he made us a
singular communication and a singular proposition.
A shipper and merchant of the place, by whom he
had often been employed, had, he said, asked him
if he was open to run a cargo of warlike stores for
the use of the Chinese soldiers in the struggle
which had just broken out, there being rumours
that the Chinamen were ill-prepared for a contest,
and badly in need of supplies. Chubb added that
he had practically closed with the offer, and was
looking about for men whom he could depend upon
to join him in the enterprise, which his employer,
foreseeing from the turn events were taking that
the Chinese ports were likely soon to be blockaded,
meant as a " feeler " to test the facilities for, and
the profit likely to arise from, the organization of a

system for supplying those munitions of war of
which the Celestials were stated to be in want,
some large orders being alleged to have been
lodged with American firms on their behalf.
Chubb was to command the vessel, and he offered
to Webster and myself the posts of first and second
hands. The remuneration was very handsome, and
we, not adverse to the prospect of a little adven-
ture, had little hesitation in closing with the proposal, much to Chubb's satisfaction, who said we
were "just the sort he wanted." His employer,
Mr. H——, I no sooner heard named, than I
remembered to have heard described as a very
keen hand, and not over-scrupulous.

The vessel which he placed at our disposal was a
screw steamer of about 2000 tons, long, low, and
sharp ; an exceedingly fast boat, capable of doing
her twenty knots an hour even when heavily laden,
as, in a desperate emergency, we were soon to find
out. Articles signed, our cargo was procured and
shipped—cannon, rifles, revolvers, cartridges, fuses,
medicines, etc., etc. We cleared without difficulty,
weighed, stood out, and laid our course straight
across the North Pacific.

Our ship, the *Columbia*, proved a beauty, in every
way fit for the risky business we were engaged
upon. Needless to say she had not only been
selected for speed, but was rendered in appearance

as unobtrusive as possible. Besides lying low in
the water, she was painted a dead grey, funnels and
all.   The sort of coal we used, anthracite, burned
with very little smoke, and even that little was
obviated, as we approached the seat of war, by a
hood on the smoke-stack.   She slipped through
the water silently and noiselessly as one of its
natural denizens, and on a dark night, with all
lights out, could hardly have been perceived, even at
a short distance, from the deck of another vessel.

Without the ship's log to refer to, I cannot be
certain of dates and distances, but it was in the
latter days of August that we were steaming up
the Yellow Sea, where, by the way, the water is
bluer than I have ever seen it elsewhere.   In some
places it presents, on a moonlit night, the appearance of liquefied ultramarine, though it certainly is
muddy enough about the coasts.   Our destination
was Tientsin, one of the most northern of the
treaty ports, and of course we kept in with the
Chinese mainland as closely as possible to avoid
the Japanese cruisers.   All had gone well, and we
were fast approaching the entrance to the Gulf of
Pechili, when we encountered one of those tempests
which are only to be met with in the Eastern seas
—pitch-black darkness, rain in one sheeted flood,
like a second Deluge, blinding flashes of forked
lightning more terrific than the gloom, and an al-

most uninterrupted crash of thunder amidst which the uproar of a pitched field would be inaudible. With our enormous steam-power we held our own for a while although unable to make much headway; but at last a tremendous sea took us right abeam on the port side; the main hatch had been left open, a small Niagara poured down it, and doused our fires. No canvas would have stood the hurricane that was blowing, and for some time we were in a serious way. Before our engines, which fortunately held firm, were working again, we had drifted helplessly over to the Corean coast, and it was all we could do to claw off-shore until the tempest abated, which it did very suddenly, as it had risen.

As the wind fell, we ran under the lee of an island, oblong, high, and thickly wooded, not far from a heavy promontory of the coast. Here we lay for two or three hours repairing damages. Of course we had no accurate idea whereabouts we had got to, but we reckoned that we could not be far from Chemulpo, a very undesirable neighbourhood from our point of view, as the port was in the hands of the Japanese, who were engaged in landing troops there, and whose armed ships would of course be in the vicinity. It was, therefore, necessary for us to spend as little time thereabout as possible. As soon as things were ship-shape once more—and luckily for ourselves we had sustained no real injury—steam was got up to regain our former course. It was already quite dark as we passed out from beneath the land ; two bells in the first night-watch, or nine o'clock, had just struck. Truly that was a case of out of the frying-pan into the fire, for no sooner had we rounded the extremity of the island than we found ourselves in most unpleasant proximity to a ship of war. I was alone on the bridge at the time, and at once caused the engines to be reversed, in the hope of slipping back behind the land from the cover of which we had just emerged. Too late ; we were perceived, and the cruiser's search-light blazed forth, illuminating the dark waters, sky, and coast-line with a vivid glare. Simultaneously we were hailed loudly, although the distance was too great to permit of the words being distinguished, keenly as I strained my ears to catch them.

Seeing that we were detected, and knowing that the appearance of flight would increase suspicion, I stopped the steamer, devoutly hoping that our unwelcome neighbour might be a detached vessel of some European squadron. That she could be Chinese there was little hope, as we were aware that the Celestial fleet was in the Gulf of Pechili. Almost before our engines were stopped, one of the cruiser's boats was in the water and dancing

towards us.   Chubb and Webster ran up from
below, and as we awaited the boat, we uneasily
speculated as to the character of the craft that
had despatched it, as she lay within a quarter of
a mile of us, the white muzzles of the guns in her
tops and turret seeming, as she rolled with the
swell, to dip in the wave.   Formidable indeed she
looked, and there was an evident stir of offensive
preparation on board her; yet in spite of our
danger, I could not resist a feeling of surprised
and wondering admiration of the wild picturesque-
ness of the scene—the majestic warship, the glitter-
ing, rolling expanse of the sea, and the black lines
of the shores, under that intense and vivid radiance,
which might fitly have emanated from one of those
phantom-craft with which maritime superstition
peoples the deep.   Everything it touched took a
ghostly and unreal look.

There was rather a heavy sea on, and the boat
took some while to reach us.   At length, however,
she was alongside, and then came clambering up
a little lieutenant, who displayed to our dismayed
vision all the physical peculiarities of the Japanese.
He addressed us in English, a language better understood than any other amongst the Mikado's subjects.

"You are American?" he asked, pointing to
the star-spangled banner on the pole-mast. "What
is the name of your vessel?"

We informed him, and received in return that of the warship, but in our consternation we paid little heed to it, and none of us could afterwards remember it. The lieutenant proceeded to question us as to our business, speaking very creditable English. We had previously agreed that in such a dilemma we should describe our cargo as consisting of salt, rice, and cloth stuffs, and we had taken the precaution to ship a quantity of those commodities, in bales and casks which were three parts full of cartridges to economize space, besides having fictitious invoices, etc. These valuable testimonials Chubb, who was outwardly as cool as ice, readily produced when the officer demanded to see our papers. He scrutinized everything carefully, and, still dissatisfied, said he would inspect our cargo. Of course we could not object, and blank indeed were our looks as the enemy walked over to the side to call up two or three of his boat's crew to assist him in the inquisition.

"Never mind," said Chubb, "it's not all up with us yet, and it won't be even if he finds out what we have aboard."

"What shall we do then?" asked Webster and I.

"Sling them overboard and run for it," said Chubb; and I knew by his determined air that he meant what he said.

"What! from under those guns?" said Webster.

There was no time for more.   The Japanese lieutenant, with his men, rejoined us, and motioned us to lead the way below.   We complied, and introduced them to our "cargo," the barrels lying everywhere three or four deep above the contraband of war.   How consuming was our anxiety as they poked about!   Things went well enough for a while; they never penetrated into the casks which they caused to be opened deep enough to find the cartridges, or hoisted out enough of them to come at what was beneath.   Our spirits were beginning to rise, when an unlucky accident sent them down to zero.   The hoops of one of the barrels handled were insecure, and coming off, the staves fell apart, and along with a defensive covering of slabs of salt, a neat assortment of revolver cartridges came tumbling out.   The Japanese lieutenant smiled till his little oblique optics were scarcely perceptible.

"Very good," said he, picking up one of the packages; "very nice—nice to eat."

We were thunderstruck, and had not a word to say.   All was up now, of course; the Japs prosecuted the search with renewed keenness, and the nature of our lading soon stood revealed.

"I shall be obliged to detain this ship, gentlemen," said the lieutenant politely, to Webster and myself.   "Where has your captain gone?"

C

I looked round for Chubb; he was not visible.

"I suppose he must have gone on deck," said I.

The lieutenant and his men hurried up, Webster and I following. Chubb was conferring with a group of the sailors. The search-light was still flaring away, and I was horrified to see that our formidable neighbour had crept up to within two or three hundred yards. The lieutenant walked sharply to the side, and shouted some directions to the boat's crew. The words were scarcely out of his mouth when I heard Chubb say, "Now." The men with whom he had been speaking rushed upon the Japanese, seized them, and in the twinkling of an eye hove them overboard into their boat, or as near it as they could be aimed in the hurry of the moment. Simultaneously "Full speed ahead" was rung from the bridge, and the steamer sprang forward as the hare springs from the jaws of the hound. For a moment there was no sound except the rush of the water foaming at the bows. Then the warship opened fire on us. Gun after gun resounded, and we held our breath as the ponderous shot hurtled past us. The first few were wide of the mark, but we were not long to go scatheless. One of the terrible projectiles struck the water by the starboard quarter, rose over the side with a tremendous ricochet, bowled over one of the men, and smashed the top of the

opposite bulwark. Immediately after another tore
transversely across the decks, playing, as Chubb
afterwards said, "all-fired smash" with everything
it encountered, and killing another of the men, who
was cut literally in two, the upper portion of his
body being carried overboard, the lower half
remaining on the deck.

"He's mad," roared Webster, meaning Chubb;
"we ain't going to be sunk to please him," and he
rushed on the bridge to put a stop to our flight.

Chubb interposed to prevent him; they closed,
grappled together, and finally fell off the bridge,
still struggling.

The cruiser had to stop to pick up her boat, and
the delay probably saved us; we must, moreover,
have been a very uncertain mark in the unnatural
light, which doubtless would be no aid to gunnery
practice. On we tore, with the steam-gauge un-
comfortably near danger point; the warship in
hot pursuit, looking, wreathed as she was in the
smoke and flame of her fiercely worked guns, and
the electric glare of the vivid shaft which still
turned night into day, more like some fabulous
sea-monster than a fabric contrived by man. She
plied us with both shot and shell; one of the latter
burst in the air over our bows; two men were
killed and several injured by the fragments. We
were struck nine or ten times in all, but they were

glancing blows, which never fairly hulled us. Chubb held on resolutely; we increased our distance fast, and at length ran out of range. Never before had I felt so thankful as when those fearful projectiles began to fall short. From that point we were safe. We were five knots better than our pursuer, and the only danger lay in the chance that some other cruiser, attracted by the firing, might be brought across the line of our flight. None, however, appeared, and our great speed dropped the enemy long before daylight.

The damage to the ship was confined to the upper works, and could soon be put to rights, but five of the crew had been killed and twice that number wounded, and unused to such work as I was, I felt strongly inclined to blame Chubb for incurring this sacrifice of life for what appeared to me an inadequate object. He laughed it away.

"They take the risk," said he, "they know it, and they are well paid for it. We've saved ship and cargo; that's all old H—— will think about, and all we need care for."

It was far, however, from being all I cared for as I looked upon the mangled corpses lately filled with life and vigour. I had embarked on the enterprise in a spirit of levity and carelessness, reflecting little on what it might entail, and there was something shocking in thus suddenly coming face to face with the dread reality of war. But whatever may have been the source of the feeling, it soon passed away, and when the dead had been sewed up in their hammocks and laid to their last rest in the deep—a ceremony we performed the day after our escape—Richard was himself again, and the old careless buoyancy swelled up once more.

Prayer-books had been omitted in our outfit, and we were at a loss for the burial service. However, we laid our heads, or rather our memories together, and most of us being able to recollect a scrap of it here and there, we contrived to patch it up sufficiently to give our unfortunate shipmates Christian burial. I should mention that another of the wounded men died after our arrival at Tientsin, and was interred in the English cemetery. He was the man who was first hit; his name was Massinger, and he claimed to be a descendant of the dramatist. He was known on board chiefly as "Hair-oil," from his addiction to plastering his bushy black hair with some shiny and odorous compound of that nature. Both his legs were broken by the shot that struck him.

As to my friend Webster, adorned with a black eye, he never ceased, during the remainder of the voyage, to declaim against Chubb's foolhardiness and uphold his own proceedings on the eventful

night. For his own discomfiture he sought con-
solation in rum, protesting that it was a miracle
that any of us had survived to taste another drop
of that liquid comforter.

"But I'm a houtcast," he would wind up invariably, as his potations overcame him; "that's
where it is—who cares what a—— houtcast thinks?"

Chubb took no further notice of him than to
laughingly threaten to put him under arrest for
mutiny. It must not be supposed that the "houtcast's" behaviour on the occasion in question was
due to any want of courage. Escape seemed impossible; the risk of the attempt was tremendous,
and I am convinced that if the matter had been
left to my own judgment, I should not have dared
it. But Chubb was one of those men whom nothing can daunt, and who are never more completely in their element than when running some
desperate hazard.

CHAPTER II

WE reached Tientsin without further mishap, and turned over our cargo to Mr. H——'s agent, who disposed of it at a handsome profit, though hardly sufficient, I thought, to warrant the risking of so valuable a ship as the *Columbia*. We lay in the port about a week, to effect the repairs rendered necessary by the Japanese gun practice.

At Tientsin a war council was sitting, and one morning Mr. Mac——, the agent, came on board and informed us that he had received a proposal for the *Columbia* to be chartered as a transport to convey troops to the Corea. It was only, he said, for an immediate special service, and the terms being exceedingly advantageous he had resolved on his own responsibility to accept the offer, as the work would not occupy us more than a few days. We were to be one of a convoy of transports which, sailing at different times from different ports, were to rendezvous in Talienwan Bay on the east coast of the Liao-tung Peninsula, where the troops

were to be embarked under protection of an armed
squadron. There was no time to be lost, and we
were to weigh anchor and make for the bay as
soon as possible.

On the afternoon of the same day two Chinese
emissaries came to make a visit of inspection, and
in the evening we steamed out of the port, flying
the American colours, with nothing of course to
fear at the moment. On arriving at Talienwan
we found the bay full of shipping. Four large
transports were already engaged in the work of
embarkation, and another arrived after we did.
The warships presented a gallant array, twelve in
all, belonging, with two or three exceptions, to the
North Coast Squadron. There were four torpedo-
boats in addition. The most powerful vessels were
the *Chen-Yuen* and the *Ting-Yuen*, barbette ships,
English-built, I think, of 7280 tons. The *King-
Yuen* and *Lai-Yuen* were two barbette ships of
smaller tonnage—2850. Then came the *Ping-
Yuen*, of 2850 tons, a coast-defence armour-clad;
a turret-ship, the *Tsi-Yuen*, of 2320 tons; the *Chih-
Yuen*, *Ching-Yuen*, *Kwang-Kai* and *Kwang-Ting*,
all of 2300 tons, deck-protected cruisers; and the
Chao-Yung and *Yang-Wei*, each of 1400 tons,
unprotected cruisers.

I have forgotten to say that we took a Chinese
agent on board at Tientsin for the trip. He was

alleged to be able to speak English, but rarely indeed was his jargon intelligible. I asked him to translate the names of the Chinese warships, but this was a task far beyond the linguistic capacity of my friend Lin Wong. I understood him to say that it would require " too muchee words " to render in our prosaic tongue the amount of poetic imagery concentrated in the expressions " Chih-Yuen," or " Kwang-Kai." Of what the names mean I am in ignorance still.

We were speedily boarded by a boat from the flagship, to the officer of which Lin Wong gave an account of his stewardship, and we received directions to draw up to the landing-stage in turn and receive our human freight. The troops were still arriving from the roads to Talien and Kinchou. They seemed for the most part an undisciplined lot, and came streaming on board in no particular order ; here and there a mounted officer directing with shouts, gestures, and blows too, the move-ments of the surging masses that crowded along the water-side. The number embarked I reckoned at about 18,000. There was also a large quantity of military stores to be shipped, and busy enough we were. In the evening I had a glimpse of Admiral Ting, who had been ashore and was returning to his ship. His barge passed close alongside the *Columbia.* I saw a young-looking

man, very pleasant in expression and manner;
altogether what we should call highly gentlemanly
in appearance.   It is well known that he expiated
his failures by suicide after the final ruin of Wei-
hai-wei.

All was complete on the second day after our
arrival, and shortly before noon the flagship signalled
us to weigh anchor.   I may remark that the Chinese
Navy is English trained, and the duty is carried on in
English, owing to the intractable character of the
Chinese language, the fact that officers and men
have thus practically to learn a foreign tongue in
order to work their ships being an obvious disadvantage.   The transports were grouped together
and the warships disposed in sections abreast and
ahead, with the active torpedo-boats in the rear.
Our destination was the estuary of the Yalu, the
large river which divides China from the Corea.
We left Talienwan on September 14, and
reached the river on the afternoon of the 16th.
The work of disembarkation commenced immediately, although rumours reached us from Wi-ju of
the disastrous defeat of the first Chinese army at
Ping-Yang in the Corea the day before.   It illus-
trates the ridiculous inefficiency of the Chinese
measures from first to last, that troops should thus
have been landed at hap-hazard far from any point
of communication with the interior of the Peninsula,

the very day after an action which extinguished their prospect of maintaining their ground in the Corea.

The warships anchored across the mouth of the river, whilst the transports proceeded some distance up the stream. Wi-ju is the only settlement of any size in this little-known region, though there are numerous fishing-hamlets scattered about. The soldiers improvised their camps along the bank. A wild scene was presented when night fell on the 16th—the glare of the bivouac, extending far along the desolate water-side; the concourse of savage figures in the lurid gloom, with here and there in the distance the gigantic shape of an illuminated warship. We worked well into the night, and were at it again when the sun rose—a glorious sunrise, pouring over everything floods of crimson splendour.

The first accounts which reached England of the action miscalled the battle of Yalu, categorically stated that it was fought off the mouth of the river whilst the work of landing the soldiers was proceeding. This story I fancy to have been invented by the Chinese as a sort of excuse for their defeat, by representing themselves as fighting at a great disadvantage in covering the disembarkation. However this may be, the fact is that the work was completed by about seven o'clock on the morning of the 17th, when no enemy was in sight. When the *Columbia* weighed and stood out of the river, after breakfast, about nine o'clock, we found that the main body of the fleet had departed, though three or four cruisers and the torpedo-boats still remained in the bay. We and the other transport masters had received an intimation that we were at liberty to return to our respective ports upon the conclusion of the work of disembarkation. As to the *Columbia*, Chubb had had instructions from Mr. H——'s agent to make straight from the Yalu to San Francisco, report to our owner, and take his further orders. We had, however, to deal with the Chinese supercargo, if I may so term him, Lin Wong, who still remained on board, and wanted to be re-conveyed to the Gulf of Pechili. We proposed to put him on board one of the warships, but as they were already under weigh when we steamed down, there was no immediate opportunity of doing so. They were following in the wake of the main squadron towards Port Arthur, steering south by west from the mouth of the river. We held on with them, only one other transport ship doing the same.

For three hours we steamed on thus, at about twelve knots. Towards noon we saw dense smoke all along the horizon ahead, and a heavy, dull, rumbling sound reached us which soon made itself

unmistakable as the roar of artillery. We immediately guessed that the squadron preceding us had
been attacked by the enemy. Our escort, if I may
so term it, drew inshore, and I at first thought from
their demeanour that they were going to shirk
entering the engagement. If such was their intention, however, they changed it, and stood boldly
on with the torpedo-boats. We came to a stop,
undecided how to proceed. The other transport
which had accompanied us was already in full
retreat, and Lin Wong, in whom discretion seemed
very unduly proportioned to valour, advised a
similar course on our part. Chubb and I, however,
felt a strong desire to see the fight, and as we were
not now under the Chinese flag, there seemed no
reason why we should not stay to witness it,
particularly as there was no need to let the
Columbia be seen.

We therefore, in spite of the unintelligible pro-
tests of Lin Wong, cast anchor, having hoisted
American colours, in one of the numerous bays that
indent the rocky coast of the Liao-tung. Then
Chubb and myself, leaving Webster in charge,
pulled off in a small boat towards the scene of
action. We kept close to the shore, and had about
a mile and a half to pull before we came abreast of
the conflict. With its deepening thunders bellow-
ing in our deafened ears, we landed where the ground

was high, and ascending the most elevated point we could perceive, had, with the aid of powerful glasses, a good view of the scene. Terrific indeed it was—a wide, dense pall of smoke, which there was little wind to carry off; through the haze the huge reeling shapes of the fighting vessels, looming indistinctly, vomiting flame like so many angry dragons, and several of them burning in addition, having been set on fire by shells; and above all the appalling concussion of the great guns, like the bursting of incessant thunder-bolts.

By this time it was half-past two p.m., and the battle had been in progress nearly three hours. Not having seen the commencement of the affair, we were for some time unable to make head or tail of it. The ships were mixed up and scattered, and we could perceive little sign of plan or combination on either side. The first thing that began to make itself evident as we watched was that the struggle was nearing the coast. At first the nearest ships had been fully a league and a half seaward; before we had occupied our position three-quarters of an hour, many were well within two miles of the coast. So evident was this that Chubb remarked that half of them would be ashore before the fighting was over. This of course enabled us to distinguish the vessels better, and we began to make out evident signs that John Chinaman was getting

much the worst of it.   The Japanese vessels, working in concert and keeping together, as we began
to perceive, seemed to sail round and round the
enemy, pouring on them an incessant cannonade,
and excelling them in rapidity of fire and manœuvring.   Some of the Chinese vessels appeared to me
to present an appearance of helplessness, and there
was no indication of combination as amongst their
opponents.   Not but what they blazed away
valiantly enough, and some of them had evidently
given as good as they got, for more than one
Japanese vessel was in flames.   Of course we could
not identify these ships, but we could make
out that in numbers and armament they were
a fair match for the Chinese squadron.   They
appeared to pay special attention to the two great
Chinese ironclads, the *Chen-Yuen* and *Ting-Yuen*,
one of which at least had had her big guns, 37-ton
Krupps, silenced, though still contributing to the
entertainment with the quick-firing armament.
Shortly after three, the *King-Yuen*, fired by shells,
began to burn fiercely; she showed through the
smoke like a mass of flame, and was evidently
sinking, settling down on an even keel.   Three or
four of the enemy circled round, plying her with
shot and shell.   Finally, with a plunge she disappeared, and the immediate darkening, as the
smoke-clouds rolled in where the fierce blaze of

the burning wreck had been, was like the sudden drawing of a veil over the spot where hundreds of men had met their simultaneous doom. The cannonade slackened, but soon broke out again fiercely as ever. About this time it seemed as if the Japanese flagship, *Matshushima*, was about to share the same fate. She looked all in a blaze forward. The fire, however, was got under, and later on she was taken out of the action.

Meanwhile the Chinese ships had been forced still nearer to the land, and the *Chao-Yung*, an absolute ruin, drifted helplessly ashore, half a league from where we stood. By the aid of our glasses we could perceive her condition clearly— her upper works knocked to pieces; her decks, strewn with mutilated bodies, an indiscriminate mass of wreck and carnage. Her crew were abandoning her, struggling to land as best they could. Subsequently the *Yang-Wei* went ashore similarly battered to pieces and burning. She was much further off, and we made her out less distinctly. On the Japanese side not one ship had sunk as far as we had seen, and though the flagship and some of the smaller craft were in an unenviable state, the attack was kept up with immense spirit, and prompt obedience was paid to signals, which were frequent, whereas we looked in vain for any sign of leadership on the part of the Celestials.

Later in the action another of their best ships, the
Chih-Yuen, came to grief. She had evidently been
for long in difficulties, labouring heavily, with the
steam-pumps constantly in requisition, as we could
tell by the streams of water poured from her sides.
Bravely she fought on unsupported, and her upper
deck and top guns were served until she sank. At
length her bows were completely engulfed ; the
stern rose high out of water, disclosing the whirl-
ing propellers, and bit by bit she disappeared. We
could hear distinctly the yelling sounds of triumph
that rose from the Japanese ships as she went
down. The *Chen-Yuen* and *Ting-Yuen*, which
seemed to fight together during the action, tried
when too late to assist her.

At five o'clock, as darkness came on, the firing
rapidly decreased, and the opposing squadrons
began to separate. Some of the Chinese vessels
were out of sight in the gloom to the southward,
and the Japanese slowly drew off seaward. We
thought it now high time to regain the *Columbia*,
and took to our boat, discussing the fight and
speculating on the probable renewal of it. We
felt little surprise that the Chinese should have had
the worst of it, for we had had good reason to suspect that their fleet had greatly fallen off from the
state of unquestionable efficiency to which English
tuition had brought it. Whilst ashore in Talien-

D

wan I had a conversation with Mr. Purvis, an English engineer on board the *Chih-Yuen*. I asked him what he thought would be the result of an encounter with an equal Japanese force. He said the Chinese would have a good chance if well handled, expressing on that head distinct doubts.

" They are very brave," said he—and I can answer for it that there was no perceptible flinching on their part during the action—" and I believe Ting to be a good man, but he is under the thumb of Von Hannecken "—meaning Captain or Major Von Hannecken, a German *army* officer, one of the foreign volunteers in the fleet. The significance of the remark is apparent when we consider the statements made to the effect that it was he who was really in command on the day of the engagement, Admiral Ting deferring to his suggestions. I am in no position to affirm whether this is really the truth or not, but if it be indeed the fact, it cannot be held to be astonishing that disaster should have overtaken a fleet manoeuvred by a *soldier!* I recollect that Mr. Purvis also informed me that the boilers of two or three of the vessels (instancing the destroyed *Chao-Yung*) were worn-out and unfit for service. Laxity of discipline, too, seems to have resulted in disobedience or disregard of orders. As an instance of this, it is alleged that instructions telegraphed from the conning-tower of the flagship were varied or suppressed by the officer at the telegraph, and that a subsequent comparison of notes with the engineer afforded proof of this.

I was forcibly struck by the comparatively unimportant part played in this action by that "dark horse" of modern naval warfare, the dreaded and much-discussed torpedo. Both squadrons had several torpedo-boats present, though, as I have shown, those on the Chinese side did not enter the action until it had been proceeding more than an hour. The Japanese allege that they did not use the torpedo at all during the action, and however this may be, there is nothing to show that the weapon made on either side a single effective hit. I drew the impression from what I saw, that it would be apt to be ineffectual as used by one ship against another, an antagonist in the evolutions of the combat, as the prospect of hitting, unless the ships were very close together, would be small. The specially-built boat, running close in, and making sure of the mark, would of course be dangerous, although the storm of shot from the quick-firing guns ought even in that case to be a tolerably adequate protection. The torpedo undoubtedly was not given a fair chance at the battle of Yalu, but the result seems to indicate that its terrors have been overrated, that artillery must still be reckoned the backbone of naval warfare. Probably the torpedo will turn out to be most effective in surprise attacks on ships and fleets at anchor. The experience of Wei-hai-wei seems to point to this.

CHAPTER III

It was dark long before we got back to the bay where we had anchored the *Columbia*, and we might have found it impossible to make out her where-abouts if Webster had not hoisted lights to guide us. When again aboard we got up steam and stood out to sea. We should have run for the Yellow Sea at once but for the presence of the Chinese agent, whom we had had no opportunity of transferring from the *Columbia*. A motion to throw him overboard was negatived, and we re-solved to hold on for Port Arthur, where we could get rid of him without going much out of our way. Besides, we felt curious to see if any further en-counter would take place between the hostile squadrons. Such, however, was not fated to be the case. The Japanese allege that they intended to renew the attack in the morning, and tried with that view to hold a course parallel with that of the retreating Chinese, but lost them during the night.

We reached Port Arthur on the 19th, and

having obtained a pilot, entered the harbour. We found there only two of the vessels belonging to the defeated squadron, the *Ping Yuen* and the *Kwang Ting*. The former did not seem much injured, but the latter had evidently suffered heavily, the port bow being partially stove, the upper works demolished, and the armouring tremendously battered and dinted.

Shortly after casting anchor in the West Port, I lowered a boat to take Lin Wong ashore. In the dockyard he ascertained that a fast steam launch was to leave for Tientsin with despatches within two days, and he arranged to take advantage of her departure to regain that port, from which, it will be remembered, he had come on board the *Columbia*. As he seemed well acquainted with Port Arthur, I got him to take me round, and show me as much of the place as could be seen in the two or three hours of leisure at my disposal, for the *Columbia* was to trip her anchor again in the evening.

The general features of Port Arthur, or, to give it its native name, Lu-Shun-Kou, must be tolerably familiar to all who have followed the course of the war. A glance at the map shows its position, at the southern extremity of the Liao-tung Peninsula, commanding, with the formidable forts of Wei-hai-wei on the opposite tongue of land, near Chefoo, the entrance to the Gulf of Pechili.

Although now the principal arsenal and naval
depôt of the Chinese Empire, it is of quite recent
creation, only having come into note since 1881, in
which year it was decided to establish a naval
dockyard. Up to then it had only been used as a
harbour for junks employed in the timber trade
and carrying cargoes from the Yalu to ports in the
Pechili Gulf, or from the south to Niuchang and
West Chin-chou. Native contractors having made
an extensive bungle of the job, it was entrusted to a
French company, and by them completed. Since
then the place has increased, from an insignificant
village of sixty or seventy mud houses and a few
shops, to a town of over a thousand dwellings, as
well as two large theatres, two temples, and a
number of banks and inns. The population at the
time of the Japanese incursion was about 5000 or
6000, in addition to a garrison of about 7000.
The port is very spacious and commodious, and
dredgers have worked assiduously for several years
past to deepen the entrance to it. The bar
has been deepened from twelve feet to about
twenty-five feet to enable permanent moorings
to be laid down for men-of-war. The dock
basin, called the East Port, covering an area of
thirty-two acres, has been constructed well behind the signal bluffs to the right of the entrance,
the West Port, or natural harbour, opening just

opposite round the long, narrow spit of land called the Tiger's Tail. The basin has a depth of twenty-five feet at low water.   There are large and numerous wharves and quays, fitted with steam cranes, and connected by a railway with the workshops, which contain all the most modern machinery and engines.   The dockyard, and in fact a considerable portion of the town, is supplied with fresh water conveyed by pipes from a spring about four miles to the north.   There is a smaller dock for torpedo boats, and a torpedo depôt on shore where those weapons can be tested and regulated.   The entrance to the port is defended by torpedoes and submarine mines, although, as I noticed, some of the latter had been so badly constructed and adjusted for depth as to show above water.

For defensive purposes nature and art have combined to render the place exceedingly strong. Ranges of hills, varying from 300 feet to 1500 feet, surround the port and town almost completely, offering scope for fortification of the most formidable character, advantages which, as far as construction goes, have been well utilized, massive and lofty stone forts occupying every point of advantage.   I believe they are of German construction.   They bristle with heavy Krupp and Nordenfeldt guns. The elevation on the coast varies from eighty feet to 410 feet.   The land defences, though newer than those seaward, are less powerful; the heaviest guns, of 21 and 24 centimetre, are in the latter. Everywhere the forts are supplemented by trenches, rifle-pits, and open redoubts or walled camps.

Such is, or was, Port Arthur, and when we remember how the Turks held Plevna, an open town until the earthworks were hastily thrown up round it, for months against all the force Russia could bring against it, one cannot but feel amazement that a place so powerful should so easily have fallen. Properly defended, it should be unreducible by anything but famine. The coast defences are impregnable, and those inland, though more susceptible of attack, should not fall before anything short of overwhelming superiority of force. I should like to have seen the 20,000 men whom the Japanese led against it take that fortress in forty-eight hours from Osman Pacha's army. The Mikado's generals, however, had formed a perfectly just estimate of their own powers as against those of the enemy. In fact, a third of their force could have taken Port Arthur from the ridiculous soldiers who held it.

The garrison in ordinary times amounts to 7000 men, but before the Japanese attack it had been increased to nearly 20,000. This is inadequate; 30,000 men at least should occupy the fortress in time of war, and 40,000 would not in my opinion be too many.

The chief man in the place when I was there was the Taotai, or governor, Kung, a brother, I have heard, of the Ambassador to England. His office, I believe, is civil; the military chiefs were Generals Tsung and Ju. The soldiers, who appeared to range about everywhere pretty much at their own discretion, were an uncouth, rough lot, with very little of the smartness of dress and bearing which we associate with the military character. Everywhere was a most portentous display of banners, as if the sacrilegious foot of a foeman could not be set on any spot rendered sacred by the dragon flag. The town presented a very neat and compact aspect, and struck me very favourably as compared with Tientsin, the only other Chinese town I had been in, and which seemed to me to be for the most part composed of narrow, dirty, stinking lanes with one or two good streets in the centre. Port Arthur, as might be expected of so recent a settlement, constructed to a large extent under European supervision, is very much better built, and altogether presents, or did present—for to a melancholy and deplorable condition was it soon to be reduced—a thriving and busy aspect.

At dusk I quitted the streets, with their bazaar-like shops and strange illuminations, and made my way back to the port under escort of my Chinese friend, who with Oriental politeness insisted on seeing me safe back on board. A most unwelcome shock awaited me. No *Columbia* was to be found, and Lin Wong's inquiries elicited that she had left nearly an hour before. We hunted up the pilot who had taken her out, and learned from him that she had steamed away south-east immediately; she could not, therefore, be awaiting me outside. What on earth could be the meaning of it? I could only conjecture that by some oversight the fact of my not being on board had been forgotten. She possibly might return on its being discovered that I had been left ashore, but in the meantime what was I to do? A suggestion by Lin solved the difficulty. If the *Columbia* did not put back, I could obtain a passage to Tientsin on the vessel which was soon to convey him to that port, where I could arrange my future proceedings according to circumstances. This seeming the only feasible plan, I, with many internal maledictions upon the stupid mischance, accompanied the agent to an hotel or inn where he had already chartered quarters for his short stay in the place. There are some half-dozen of these establishments in Port Arthur. Three or four of them are wretched hovels, which existed in the squalid infancy of the town; the newer ones are larger and fairly commodious and comfortable. The one we occupied was near one of the gates of the approaches to the north-eastern forts. Mine host was a square, thick-set Celestial named Sen. Port Arthur being well accustomed to " foreign devils," some of the servants had been engaged for their knowledge of that curious dialect " pidgin English," which in the far East is pretty much what Lingua Franca is in the Levant. With a little practice it is easily comprehended, although, under the chaperonage of Lin, my difficulties were largely reduced. Fortunately I had a considerable sum of American money in my pockets, and with Lin's aid was able to negotiate it at one of the banks, at a pretty smart loss, I may say. Otherwise I was fairly content and comfortable, and had no human want but whisky.

CHAPTER IV

NOTHING of interest occurred during the day and a half that elapsed before the departure of the despatch-boat. Punctual enough as to time she steamed out of the harbour under cover of night, with the Chinese agent and myself on board. Misfortunes are well known never to come singly, and so it was in my case. The morning after our departure was very foggy, and towards noon we had to slow down to less than half speed. Suddenly, without a moment's warning, a Japanese gunboat loomed through the dun vapour close on the port bow. With their ridiculous fondness for showing it on all occasions, in season and out, the Celestials had their flag flaunting on a staff in the stern. The Japanese on the gunboat perceived it, for without troubling to hail she opened on us with the machine-guns in her tops. A storm of balls swept the deck, and half of those upon it fell dead or wounded. One of the bullets cut off the peak of my cap with mechanical neatness, leaving the rest of the article on my head, though turned quite round, back to front. Before anything could be done to increase our speed, a quick-firing gun plumped several heavy shot through us. The machinery was damaged, we swung round helplessly, and were evidently fast sinking. We had two boats of no great size; one of them was knocked to splinters by the shot; the other we lowered as fast as we could. As many as it would hold got into it, the others jumped into the water, and within half a minute afterwards our vessel went down, and the woe-begone survivors of the sudden catastrophe found themselves prisoners on the deck of her destroyer.

She was the *Itsuku* gunboat of about five hundred tons, on a cruise of observation in the Gulf, along with two or three consorts, whom she had lost in the fog. There was not a soul on board who could speak a word of English, but by a few Chinese was sufficiently understood, and a gunnery officer could speak tolerable French, a knowledge of which tongue I shall probably be recollected to have mentioned as being the major portion of the inadequate exchange for my eighty thousand pounds. They informed us that they had taken us for a torpedo boat, and seeing the Chinese flag had no hesitation in opening fire on so dangerous a neighbour, as they deemed us. They seemed very scantily pleased when told our real character, and learnt that their precipitancy had perhaps lost them a little promotion, or at least honourable mention, as capturers of important despatches, as I understand them to have been.

I remained on board this vessel for more than a month. The Chinese, of course, were prisoners of war, but there was no ground for detaining me as such. I related how I had been left behind by the *Columbia* at Port Arthur, without, of course, giving any hint that she had been engaged in supplying China with war material. I thought this would satisfy my captors, but I was not long in finding out that they entertained their own ideas as to my character, for one day I was plainly asked whether I was not a military or naval instructor of the Chinese. I was able to conscientiously deny that I was any such thing, but the query took me very much aback, as the naturalness of the suspicion was obvious, and I foresaw no end of trouble in clearing myself of it. The commander of the gunboat, a consequential and rather surly personage, shook his head, and said he would have to take time to consider the matter.

Time he certainly did take, and plenty of it. We were, however, well treated, chiefly through the kindness of the French-speaking officer, Lieutenant Hishidi, with whom I struck up an acquaintance, he being in fact the only one of the gunboat's crew with whom I could converse. He caused a small separate cabin to be extemporized for myself and Lin Wong, and looked to our comfort in other ways. My friend Lin, I should say, had received a nasty graze on the ribs of the right side from one of the machine-gun bullets, but otherwise was all right, though in a very chop-fallen condition at being made prisoner. He and I were allowed more liberty than the other captives, and apart from the detention had little to complain of.

I was naturally much interested at first in looking round me and taking stock of the Japanese sailors and their vessel. She was in superb fighting trim, beautifully clean and well found in every part, and the duty was carried on with thorough man-of-war smartness. It was impossible to watch these little active, clever, determined sailors without feeling that the men of the finest navy in the world, which I take to be that of her Britannic Majesty, would find in them foemen worthy of their steel. I remember that they were daily exercised at the guns, and the promptitude and precision with which they sank the *Kowtung*—such was the unlucky despatch-boat's name—was a handsome testimonial to the accuracy of their aim.

Lieutenant Hishidi and I had many conversations, chiefly during his watches, and our talk generally turned on the war and nautical matters. Of the Chinese he spoke with unmeasured contempt, certainly not undeserved, and said that the Japanese fleets and armies had no misgiving as to the result of the struggle ; they felt able, against such opponents, to do anything and go anywhere— "aussi loin que mer et terre puissent nous mener," was his emphatic expression.

"We have been making this war for a long time," said he, "and we feel sure of what we can do."

I remarked on the extraordinary rapidity with which a nation, closed like the Japanese, up to within thirty years since, to European trade and European ideas, had adopted and assimilated the system of Western civilization.

"Yes," he replied, "we can learn, and we have learnt, because we saw that the knowledge would give us a great advantage in our own part of the world."

He had been in France, and expressed great admiration of French ship-building and French seamanship, and seemed doubtful when I maintained that British seamen would in case of war assert their superiority over the French ones just as decisively now as they ever had done in the past —and of naval history in general Hishidi had a good idea.

E

"You might," he said, "as your navy is so much larger than theirs."

But I pointed out that our naval triumphs had seldom been gained by superior force—"although," I admitted, "we certainly have now double the force of any other European power, on which account none of them dare attack us singly, as they know that if they did, the majority of their knocked-out tubs would be towing up the Downs in a very brief space of time. But numbers apart, the British sailor of to-day can still do more with a ship than a Frenchman. The conditions are certainly completely changed, but the best seaman will make the most of the new order."

He shook his head dubiously, and said he should like to see a war between England and France.

"Well," said I, "you may live to see that and not be an old man. You may live to see a war between England and half the rest of the world, and see England get the best of it. It has happened once or twice before."

On another occasion we were talking about Russia, when Hishidi remarked—

"Russia wants China."

"Russia wants everything," said I.

"Ah, that is what they say of you," replied he.

I once asked him what he thought of the torpedo.

"Well," said he, " the torpedo is as yet far from being thoroughly understood. It is very uncertain in use, though when it takes effect invariably deadly. Gun-fire should be able to neutralize it, that is, to keep it at a distance, for once struck, no sort of construction could resist the explosion of two hundred pounds of gun-cotton against the hull under the water line; water-tight compartments would be of no avail against such devastation. Vessels of the cruiser type, fast, and with a heavy quick-firing armament, are best suited to cope with torpedo-boats, which would find it difficult to get to close quarters with such craft. Warships have lately been built with a considerable increase of length, which of course increases a torpedo's chance of striking by giving it a larger target. Moderate size, no overloading with armour, speed, good coal supply, and as many quick-firing guns as can be mounted—that is my idea of the best type of war-ship at present. The policy of building monstrous ships is doubtful, when they can be sunk by a torpedo-boat. Under such conditions, it seems to me that ease and rapidity of manœuvring is of more advantage than gigantic weight of ordnance and armour, because after all the torpedo's attack is directed against a part which nothing can render invulnerable."

Such is the substance of my conversation with

the lieutenant, but despite the charms of intel-
lectual intercourse, I soon began to get desperately
weary of my detention. Day after day the *Itsuku*
cruised about, sometimes in company with other
craft, sometimes alone. The enemy kept well out
of sight, and few events occurred to chequer the
monotony. Once we sighted two Chinese gun-
boats not far from Chefoo, and the Japanese varied
the day's drill and gun exercise by shelling them
into Wei-hai-wei. They ran ignominiously and
never made the least show of fight. Had the
Itsuku been a faster vessel, she would undoubtedly
have captured or destroyed one of them. Her
maximum speed was under sixteen knots. On
another occasion, off the western coast of the Liao-
tung, we came upon a fleet of junks, craft engaged
in coast trade, I presume. Their crews ran them
ashore and escaped, whilst the Japanese fired the
stranded junks with shells, the officers amusing
themselves by sighting the guns and betting on
the shots. When a satisfactory bonfire had been
created we steamed away.

This sort of thing, I have said, went on for more
than a month. The gunboat's cruising-ground was
chiefly about the mouth of the Pechili Gulf, now
under the frowning forts of Wei-hai-wei, and now
opposite Port Arthur on the other side. There did
not seem to be any regular blockade of the Gulf,

though Japanese warships were constantly hovering about. The Chinese fleet, I believe, confined itself to the modest seclusion of Wei-hai-wei harbour, and was not to be tempted outside. Once I asked Hishidi when they meant to assail Wei-hai-wei and Port Arthur?

"Oh," said he, "we are waiting our time; it has not come yet."

British war-vessels were frequently in sight, but to my requests to be put on board one of them, or at least to be brought before a Japanese admiral, the commander of the *Itsuku*—I have completely forgotten his name—turned a deaf ear. October wore away, and any termination of my captivity seemed as distant as ever. I was obliged to put an end to it on my own initiative. One evening —the fourth or fifth of November it would be—we were outside Port Arthur. At dusk the gunboat anchored, and a boat was despatched on some errand of reconnaissance. A point of the coast was less than a mile distant, and as I leant over the bulwark in the fore-part of the vessel, it struck me that I might easily swim off to it, if I could get into the water unobserved. Under Webster's tuition I had become an excellent swimmer. I looked round; I was apparently not under notice, and there was no light near where I was. My mind was made up at once. I stole as far forward as I could, and watching

my opportunity, and steadying myself by the
cathead, I made a leap for the cable, intending to
climb down it to the water. A leap in the dark
is proverbially a dangerous thing; the vessel per-
versely veered away as I sprang, and instead of
catching the cable I soused into the water with a
loud splash. The sentry on the gangway heard it,
ran forward, and emptied the magazine of his rifle
at me as I swam away, but by diving and swimming under water out of the direct line of advance,
I managed to evade the bullets. A boat was soon
down and in hot pursuit, but I had had a good
start, and they were at a loss for my true direction
at first. I struck out vigorously and made good
headway, but had the disadvantage of swimming
in my clothes; moreover, the water was frightfully
cold, and began to chill me to the bone. I could
tell, however, that the tide was strongly in my
favour, and I believe I should have escaped the
boat's notice, but that the people on shore, hearing,
I suppose, the rifle-shots, turned on an electric
search-light to see what was going forward. I was
still a good quarter of a mile from the shore, and
the boat was nearly as close in—almost parallel
with me, though several hundred yards away.
There was no fort near, but I could see the dark
mass of one on a towering height far to the left.
The bright glare soon showed me to my pursuers,

who turned the boat's head towards me and gave
way with might and main.   They closed fast, and
I gave myself up for lost.   A heavy rifle-fire began
crackling along the shore, and the balls frequently
skimmed along the water disagreeably near me.   I
struggled on, but would inevitably have been re-
taken if the event had depended on my own efforts.
There was a small coast battery near containing
two or three mortars, and a shell was thrown at the
boat as it held its daring course for the shore.   It
was not a hundred yards from me at the moment.
I heard the scream of the projectile, saw it describ-
ing its flaring parabola in my direction, and with
my last energies dived to avoid it.   The sound of
its explosion rang in my ears as I went under.
When I came up again, the boat was putting
back in a hurry with three or four oars disabled.
How near to them the bomb had pitched I cannot
say, but they had evidently got a good allowance
of the splinters, though chance probably had more
to do with the matter than marksmanship.   The
gunboat was under steam and standing in, returning the fire.   I strained every nerve, and struggled
ashore at last in such a numbed and exhausted
state that I could not stand upright without assist-
ance.   I found myself surrounded by Chinese
soldiers, who plied me with questions, which I
could not have answered even if I had understood

Chinese. Perceiving my condition, they took me off to a small building like a guard-house, some way to the rear of a line of trenches. They made a blazing wood fire in the middle of the stone floor, and when I had stripped off my wet clothes and was partially thawed, they renewed their interrogatories. I absolutely knew not a word of Chinese, and could only endeavour by gestures to give them an idea of what had happened. This was not very satisfactory, but they at least could make out that I was no friend to the Japanese. They jabbered away for a while amongst themselves, apparently discussing me. At length one of them brought me some food in a large wooden bowl—a strange mess of I know not what mysterious compounds, amongst which, however, I could distinguish rice. It was palatable and I ate it gladly, and asked, too, for a supplementary supply, which was not denied. Overcome by exhaustion and the fierce heat of the fire, a drowsy stupor came upon me, and I made signs that I wished to sleep. They did not seem to have any clothing to offer me for my own which was drying in the blaze, but they brought in several long, coarse cloaks or mantles, and one of them enveloping himself in these, stretched himself before the fire on the ground, to intimate to me that in such a manner I must pass the night. Another offered me a pipe of opium, which I knew it would

be a great discourtesy, according to their ideas, to
decline, although I was quite unaccustomed to the
drug.   I therefore took it and affected to smoke,
and as I lay down, they left the little room in
which they had placed me, and I heard them
barricade the door outside.

I immediately fell into a profound slumber.
The few whiffs of opium which, despite of myself,
I had inhaled, had their effect, and produced a
series of those magical dreams with which the
drug tempts and deceives the novice.   Through
all of them the idea of flight and pursuit ran
bewilderingly.   I will give one as a specimen.   I
dreamt that I was on the shore of the sea; the
waters suddenly began to rise, and threatened
to overwhelm me.   I turned and ran, but nearer
and nearer the flood came after.   Then there
yawned across my path a precipice of which I
could not see the bottom.   Down I plunged.   I
seemed to fly like a bird, and once more stood on
firm ground.   The precipice seemed to reach to
the sky behind me.   I resumed my flight, and
looking back, beheld the flood leaping down the
gulf in a mighty volume, with the sun rising above
it, and bathing the illimitable cataract with golden
light.   It would be impossible to describe or
imagine the gorgeousness of the spectacle.   With

such visions as these does the treacherous narcotic lure its victims. I believe its use is forbidden by the Chinese military authorities, but the undisciplined soldiers seemed to use it extensively when they could get it, like tobacco.

CHAPTER V

I SLEPT till the middle of the following day, and would in all probability have slept longer but that I was awakened by my hosts, if so I may term them. My clothes were quite dry; I got into them, and was escorted outside at once. The first thing I saw was a detachment of cavalry, mounted on little shaggy Tartar ponies. One of these I was invited to bestride, and a moment afterwards, without the possibility of explanations being either asked or given, we were *en route*.

I may as well say at once that the spot where I had come ashore was the land below the West Port, and I was being conveyed to the Man-tse-ying fort, one of the principal seaward fortifications. It has an elevation of 266 feet above the sea level, and the latter part of the ascent had to be made on foot. I was at once taken before the commandant, who with a few other officers and a secretary sat prepared to investigate the peculiar circumstances which had brought a Fan Quei, or foreign devil, amongst them. The secretary knew English very indifferently—so indifferently that I am doubtful if he understood my story rightly. He asked me if I was acquainted with German, and gave me to understand that he knew more of that language than of English; however, I did not know ten words of it. The examination was long, and, from the difficulty of understanding one another, confused enough. I gathered that I was, or had been, under suspicion of being a Japanese spy in the minds of those before whom I had been brought, and they rigorously questioned the men whom I had first seen as to the circumstances attending my landing. These, I consoled myself by reflecting, could not be deemed consistent with the supposition that I was an agent of the enemy. I was asked if there was any one in the town who could witness to my having been there previously under the circumstances I alleged. I replied that probably the people at the inn would remember me.

Finally the Chinamen held a lengthened consultation amongst themselves, at the end of which I was told that I would be taken forthwith before the higher authorities on the other side of the port. I hinted to the secretary that I had had nothing to eat that day and felt decidedly hungry. I was accordingly served before my departure with a meal of fish and boiled bread, with a cup of rice wine, a decoction which tasted like thin, sour claret. This done, I was placed in charge of my former escort, who struck across country from the rear of the Man-tse-ying, passed two or three other forts and numerous entrenchments and redoubts, and finally reached the water on the inner side of the long arm of land enclosing the West Port. Here, close by a torpedo store, I was put on board a sampan, a long, narrow boat, sharp at both extremities, with an awning. In this I was conveyed to the East Port and taken through the dockyards to the military head-quarters near the great drill and parade ground at the entrance to the town. It was late in the evening when we arrived there, and I was not brought up for examination until the next day. Here, to my great satisfaction, I found I had to deal with somebody who knew English well—a military aide-de-camp, who spoke the language with both fluency and correctness. To him I told my story plainly and straightforwardly, and by the testimony of my former landlord, Sen, and an official at the bank where I had changed my money, established my identity as the person who had passed two days in the town with Wong, and accompanied him on board the despatch-boat. This was sufficient to procure my release. Everything I said was very carefully noted down. My interrogation was conducted before a couple of mandarins. The Taotai I believe to have been absent from the place at this time. He is alleged to have deserted his position and to have been ordered back again. This may or may not be so, but it is undoubtedly the fact that he fled from Port Arthur the night before the Japanese attacked it. He does not appear to have been open to the accusation of heroism.

I was informed by the aide-de-camp that the port had been visited only a day or two before by the British warship *Crescent*, the officers of which had landed for a short while. Fate seemed resolved that I should have no chance of leaving the place without seeing in it something worth remembering, as I had no sooner returned to Sen's inn, which I did on my release, than I was seized with a kind of aguish fever, the effect, no doubt, of the exposure I had recently undergone. It was nothing serious, but caused a feeling of great lassitude and depression, and confined me indoors for some ten or twelve days. I had the place almost to myself, as the approach of the Japanese armies had not been favourable to custom, and the usual course of travel to and from the north had been suspended. Sen was anxious to learn from me whether I considered it advisable for residents and townspeople to leave the port. I replied, as I sincerely thought, that the Japanese, if they succeeded in taking the place, would do no harm to non-combatants. I was, however, fatally mistaken.

The inn was a place of two storeys—few Chinese habitations have more. Most of the rooms opened round a partially covered courtyard. I had a good one in the upper storey, or the "top-side," as it is expressed in "pidgin." There were no fireplaces ; the apartments were chiefly warmed by charcoal in braziers. Along one side of that which I occupied was a long low hollow bench, filled with hot air from a furnace. This contrivance usually served me for a bed, for although they use bedsteads, there is nothing on them but an immense wadded quilt, in which you roll yourself up. I transferred it to the hot-air holder, which made a far warmer and more comfortable couch. I was waited on mostly by a lad named Chung, one of the professors of "pidgin." He was a native of Canton, had been in Hong Kong, and was well accustomed to Englishmen and their ways. The fare was very tolerable—poultry, pork, and various kinds of fish, but no beef, as the Chinaman deems it wrong to kill the animal that helps to till the ground. Chung told me that in the south cats and dogs are fattened for food, which it occurred to me would be a distinct advantage in Port Arthur at that time, with a siege imminent, and a great abundance of those animals observable. For drink I naturally had plenty of tea, though it is very washy stuff as made by the Chinese, who usually content themselves with putting the leaves in a cup and pouring hot water over them, flavouring the infusion with tiny bits of lemon.

As soon as I was sufficiently recovered to go out, I made an effort to find out whether there was any prospect of getting away from the place by sea, but soon found that this was hopeless to expect. No foreign vessels were in the port, and the native ones were chiefly junks, the proprietors of which, as interpreted by Chung, whom I took with me, refused to venture out unless for such a sum as I could by no possibility procure. There were no Chinese war-vessels in the harbour, and indeed they would have been of no use there.

Knowing that the fortress was a very strong one, I made up my mind that there would be a protracted siege, and my spirits fell as I surveyed the prospect, for my pecuniary resources were limited, and it seemed very unlikely that I would again see the *Columbia* in the port. However, my fears were groundless. Little did I think that within three days the place would be in the hands of the Japanese.

It was on November 18 that I made the fruitless attempt to negotiate for a passage. The appearance of the place had considerably changed

since first I was in it.   The numbers of the soldiery
had obviously been largely increased.   Industry
was completely suspended in the dockyard, the
whole of which had been converted into barracks.
In returning from the wharves with Chung, I
witnessed a specimen of military punishment.
Passing the open gate of an enclosure near the
clearing-house, I perceived a group which at once
riveted my attention.   A number of soldiers were
standing round one who, stripped to the waist, was
kneeling with his forehead stooped almost to the
ground, and his hands tied behind, the thongs that
bound them being held by a man standing close in
his rear.   Thus disposed, he received a tremendous
flogging from a whip with a fearful heavy leathern
lash, which made me think of the Russian knout.
The blows fell with a thud that made my
nerves shiver, and the back of the sufferer was
covered with blood, which was thrown here and
there by the ensanguined instrument of torture as
it whistled through the air.   He took his punishment, however, to use the language of the P.R., like
a man, and though his body seemed to bend like a
reed with each stroke, he never uttered a sound
that I could hear.   I did not count the lashes, but
there was no stint in the allowance.   Minute after
minute the castigator laboured away in his vocation,
until finally the victim collapsed, and rolling over,

F

lay like a log in a pool of blood, and was then carried off. I was rather surprised to see a whip used, as I had always supposed the bastinado to be the favourite method of flagellation in China. I asked Chung for an explanation, but he did not seem to understand my question, and replied that the " one piecee ting (soldier) no hab muchee hurtee," and that they might if they had liked have cut off his " one piecee head." True it is that decapitation is a very common punishment in the Chinese army.

Strongly as the massacre by the Japanese troops in Port Arthur is to be condemned, there is not the slightest doubt in the world that the Chinese brought it on themselves by their own vindictive savagery towards their enemies. The attacking armies, advancing down the Peninsula in touch with the fleet, were now within a day or two's march of the inland forts. Bodies of Chinese troops harassed and resisted them, and brushes between the opposing forces frequently took place. The Chinese took some prisoners, whom they slew mercilessly, and one of the first things I saw on the morning of the 19th was a pair of corpses suspended by the feet from the branches of a huge camphor tree near the parade-ground. They were hideously mutilated. They had been disembowelled; the eyes were gouged out, the throat cut, and the right hand severed. They were perfectly naked, and groups of children were pelting them with mud and stones.

Similar ghastly spectacles were to be seen in other parts, both inside the town and beyond it. Nor was this the worst ; the walls exhibited placards, in the sacred imperial yellow, inciting to these atrocities. This I know by means of Chung, whom I usually took out with me. The tenor, as he translated, was this :—" To the soldiers and subjects of the Celestial Lord of the Dragon Throne. So much for every Japanese dog alive. So much for his head or hand. In the name of the Sacred Son of Heaven," etc. Then came the date and the signature of the Taotai. The exact amount of the rewards I forget. I think it was fifty taels for a live prisoner, and a less amount for heads or hands. The bodies of the Japanese soldiers killed in encounters with the enemy as they closed on the place, were often found minus the head or right hand, sometimes both, besides being ferociously gashed and slashed. Corpses were still hanging on the trees when the fortress fell, and it is not surprising that their former comrades should have been maddened by the sight, though of course the officers are greatly to blame for permitting the fearful retaliation which ensued to be carried to such lengths. The massacre seems to have been allowed to continue unchecked until no more victims could be found.

This, however, is to anticipate. On the 19th the enemy were close upon the forts, and everything was bustle and commotion. Business was suspended nearly everywhere, and the movements of the troops were the chief attraction. Great crowds gathered in the vicinity of the general's pavilion overlooking the parade-ground, where a council was held in the afternoon. A strong armed force held back the mob. All the principal military officers arrived from their posts at the head of their staffs one by one. The Taotai was brought from his residence in a magnificent sedan-chair, carried by ten or twelve bearers. The pavilion itself is a splendid structure, adorned with the most gaudy and brilliant colours, and covered with Chinese characters beautifully worked in gold. The consultation lasted for at least three hours. I had only a distant view of Kung over the heads of the soldiers. The fighting outside continued, and on the next day more Japanese corpses had been brought in by the vengeful soldiery, and left for the rabble to amuse themselves with. I do not think that any Japanese was brought into the town alive.

Towards noon the next day (20th) the first guns were heard. Cannon rumbled away in the distance

all the afternoon, ceasing as night came on. A
wild and anxious night it was. There was no
certain news of the fighting, and the most contra-
dictory rumours were prevalent. Excited crowds
filled the streets, which blazed with great coloured
paper lanterns, of which nearly every individual
carried one; indeed, the person who is seen outside
without a lantern after dark becomes an object of
suspicion to the police watch.

I determined to see, if possible, something of the
fighting next day. All the ground around Port
Arthur is, as I have before remarked, very hilly.
Outside the town, and between it and the north-
western forts, is a lofty elevation named White
Boulders, for an obvious reason—the ground is full
of chalk. This spot I determined upon as my
point of observation. Most of the front face had
been covered with trenches, but the rear was easy
of attainment, and I was struggling up the steep
ascent at day-break. The summit is very uneven,
covered with huge crags and deep indentations, and
there were any number of secure enough nooks to
pick and choose from.

The field of action seen from White Boulders is
very simple and may be described in a few words.
Behind me was the West Port; on my left the
north-western fortifications, called the Table Mountain forts; on my right the East Port and the sea,

and in front the greater part of the town, with the north-eastern forts beyond. Of these latter there are, I think, eight, all connected by a wall. I had only a partial view of them. Between the elevations on which stand the north-eastern and north-western forts, the ground sinks deeply, and there is a wide space comparatively level, part of it occupied by a village. This tract is defended by redoubts and earthworks, and can be swept by the fire of the higher fortifications, particularly by those of the north-east, but still it is a weak point in the defence, though capable, it seemed to me, of being greatly strengthened.

The day broke with a frosty clearness, and though I had no glass, it was possible to see for miles on every hand. The dragon flag waved everywhere on the Chinese forts, but I could see at first no sign of the Japanese, and it was not until they began to fire that their positions were indicated. It was about half-past seven when, far to the north-west, their guns began to boom. All their preparations had apparently been made over-night, and they were only waiting for daylight to begin. The Chinese opened fire in reply on both sides; battery after battery joined in, and soon there was a thundering roar of artillery, and a dense volume of white smoke, through which glanced the flash of the cannon, all round the great semi-circle. The scream of shells, and the blaze and detonation with which they burst, were incessant. Away on the right the sea was covered with warships, which seemed to have nothing to do, and certainly were not assailing the coast defences. Some of the seaward forts were able to get their guns to bear on the positions of the Japanese armies, and were blazing away, though I don't think they could do much damage.

Some minor outlying fortifications had been captured the previous afternoon, and the Japanese had divided into two bodies for the main assaults on the north-west and north-east. The Chinese in these two sections appeared to have no combination, and by a feint at the north-east the Japanese kept that part diverted until the west forts had been carried. It is a fact that they fell about an hour and a half after the cannonade commenced. The Japanese infantry advanced against them, and the valiant troops holding them ran away at the sight. The Chinese forts on the other side now began to fire away across the intervening valley, as if that could remedy the disaster. Upon them then became concentrated the whole Japanese fire. The Chinamen here made a far better show, and the fire was vigorous and sustained. About eleven o'clock, with a terrific blast of flame and thunder, which seemed to shake the ground far and near to the

shores of the sea, their largest fort, the Shoju, or
Pine Tree Hill, blew up ; a shell must have alighted
in the magazine. At noon the whole Japanese line
advanced to the charge, and here, too, the Celestials
never waited for the assault, but fled precipitately.
There was no fighting at all at close quarters; not
a solitary Chinaman stood for a bayonet thrust.
Thus pusillanimously were abandoned these two
great masses of fortifications, placed in the most
commanding situations, on steep mountain heights
where attacking forces could keep no sort of regular
formation, and could have been mowed down in
thousands by competent gunners as they struggled
up the impregnable inclines. It was with a feeling
of bewilderment that I beheld such powerful
defences lost in such a manner, and realized that
after three or four hours' bombardment on one
side, without a shot fired against the tremendous
coast defences, it was all up with Port Arthur.

The victors next turned their attention to the
redoubts and walled camps on the lower ground,
with the calm method which distinguished all their
operations. From the valleys between the hills
began to emerge dark columns of infantry, which
closed steadily upon the devoted town, rolling to
their positions with the mechanical regularity of
parade, the sheen of their bayonets glancing here
and there through the volumes of smoke which had

settled thickly in the hollows. Nearer, spread over the ground to which the forts their cowardice had lost should have afforded ample protection, were the disorganized masses of Chinese, preparing for their last scattered and fruitless efforts. Only one of the inland forts, that nearest to the town, and called, I think, Golden Hill, was still in their possession. The trenches below me on White Boulders' front face, which had been unoccupied during the early portion of the day, now began to swarm with riflemen, whose weapons kept up a continuous roll, swelled from many a rifle-pit and redoubt away forward from the base of the elevation. Steadily the enemy advanced, working their way round on both wings within the captured fortresses. They took skilful advantage of every protection the ground afforded, and the resistance in their front rapidly diminished as they pressed on irresistibly from position to position.

It was now high time for me to evacuate my post, where I had had a solitary and secure vantage-place amidst the rugged inequalities of its summit, which probably I should not have been permitted to attain if I had not set about it so early. Past its front runs a shallow but broad stream, which coming through the Suishiyeh valley, rounds the parade-ground on the south towards White Boulders, whence it flows into a large and deep creek farther west. This stream the Japanese had to cross before they could attack the trenches below me. Two or three times they were beaten back by the hail of bullets poured on them at very close range, but covered by a heavy fire on their own side they were at length over, and then their opponents took to flight round the right-hand side of the hill. I stayed only to see this, and plunged down the rear. It was growing dusk, and I had numerous narrow escapes of breaking my neck in the deep and rugged hollows, some of them almost ravines, which seam that side of the elevation.

The town was now at the mercy of the con-querors. The Chinese were running from the Golden Hill fort as I descended, without an effort at defending it, and the water beyond was covered with boats and small craft filled with fugitives, mostly the dastardly troops, who threw away arms and uniforms as they ran. For incompetence and cowardice commend me for the future to Chinese soldiers. The twenty thousand of them who occu-pied Port Arthur contrived to kill about sixty of their antagonists on November 21, with all the best modern weapons at their disposal. And these are the men who, according to Lord Wolseley and other critics, are some day to start out to conquer the earth! Let, says Lord Wolseley, a Napoleon arise amidst this vast people, and we shall see.

But is an essentially unwarlike nation at all likely
to breed a Napoleon, or to supply him with open-
ings for a career? Who ever heard of a Chinese
conqueror? Have they ever appeared otherwise
than as the most self-centred and unenterprising
people in the world, displaying the least possible
aptitude for the career of arms? And from what
source, after thousands of years of such character-
istics, are they to bring forth the material for this
sudden burst of conquering militarism?

CHAPTER VI

I DIRECTED my retreat towards the dockyards, with a view to getting round to the south part of the town, as far as possible from the quarter by which the Japanese were entering it. The idea of a general massacre never entered my mind, and I only thought of getting back to my inn, there to stay until things quieted down. My prevailing feeling was one of satisfaction that I should not after all have to face a long residence in a beleaguered town. I therefore paid little attention at first to the fact that people were flying on every hand, and I did not suppose that there could be any good reason for flight, beyond the desirability of getting out of the way of the conquering troops until the ardour of victory had cooled down. I was not long to be left undeceived. A deadly work of vengeance and slaughter had commenced Down the panic-crowded streets, louder and louder as I advanced, came ringing the volleys of the rifle-fire, the shouts of the infuriated soldiers, and the

death-shrieks of their victims. I knew that all
armed resistance had been broken, and as these
sounds of terror increased, an idea of what might
be imminent crossed my mind. I recollected what
so often follows the fall of a place carried by
storm; I remembered the atrocities committed on
the Japanese prisoners; and I remembered, too,
the general character of all Oriental soldiers. I
paused to consider my situation. I had passed
round by the water-side until outside the dock
basin, and then turned into the streets, striking
across in the direction of the inn, with the route
from which to the East Port I was well enough
acquainted. There was a rush and hurry of
fugitives all around me, and now for the first time
I saw the Japanese soldiers in pursuit, pressing on
the fleeing throng, and using rifle and bayonet
furiously on all and sundry, stabbing and
hacking fiendishly at those who fell. I was
knocked down in the rush and trampled upon,
and it was some time before I could rise. A
Japanese soldier was near me as I staggered to
my feet, and took aim at me with his rifle. The
barrel was within a foot of me, and I struck it
aside just in time to escape getting a bullet through
my body. I had no weapon but those of nature,
but in their use I was, like most of the Anglo-
Saxon breed, something of an artist, and before

the Jap could recover his piece I gave him a good, straight, British right-hander between the eyes, which sent him down like a nine-pin. In all human probability it was the first sample of the article that had ever come under his notice; he was clearly unused to the method of attack, and lay quite flat as if to think it over, whilst I re-treated as fast as my legs could carry me. I resolved to hold on for the inn, thinking that if I succeeded in reaching it, I should be comparatively safe, as perhaps the outbreak of fury might confine itself to the streets. I knew, too, that I had not much farther to go. I made little progress, never-theless, being frequently turned out of the road by the necessity of avoiding the soldiers, who were spreading fast across the town, shooting down all whom they encountered. One began to stumble over corpses in nearly every street, and the risk of encountering parties of the murderers increased every minute. Again and again I came into the midst of the work of butchery, and every now and then ran the gauntlet of a flight of bullets fired down the narrow avenues. At length I lost my way completely, and wandered about through the pandemonium around, thinking that each minute would be my last. At length, in emerging from a dark lane leading up an ascent, I came upon a sheet of water. I immediately recognized it as a

large shallow fresh-water lake in the rear of the
dock basin, and it thus appeared that I had strayed
back nearly to the point where I had re-entered
the town on descending from White Boulders.

A frightful scene was before me. I have said
that the land by which I had come out on the
lake inclined steeply upwards, and the water was
about fifteen feet below me when I arrived in sight
of it. It was surrounded by crowds of Japanese
soldiers, who had driven large numbers of the
fugitives into the water, and were firing on them
from every side, and driving back with the bayonet
those who attempted to struggle out. The dead
floated on the water, which was reddened with
blood. The soldiers, yelling and laughing with
vengeful glee, seemed to gloat over the agonies of
their victims. It was fearful to see those gory
forms struggling in the agitated water, those who
still lived endeavouring to extricate themselves
from the mass of corpses, falling fast, but often
rising again with their last energies, streaming
with water and blood, and uttering piteous cries
and appeals for mercy, which were mocked by the
fiends around them. Many women were amongst
them; one I noticed carrying a little child, which,
struggling forward, she held up to the soldiers as
if in appeal. As she reached the bank, one of the
wretches struck her through with his bayonet, and

with a second stroke as she fell transfixed the child, which might have been two years old, and held its little body aloft.   The woman rose and made a wild effort to regain the child, but evidently exhausted and dying, fell back again into the water.   Her body—and in fact it was done with every body that came within reach—was hacked in pieces.   Fresh batches of victims were being driven in, until there threatened soon to be no room in the water for any more.   I could bear the spectacle no longer, but turned and fled from the ghastly spot.

I now knew my whereabouts, and once more set out for the inn, along the line from which I had strayed.   Heaps of dead and spectacles of murder were continually presenting themselves.   In one place I saw some ten or twelve soldiers with a number of unfortunates whom they had tied back to back in a batch.   With volley after volley they despatched them, and proceeded to mutilate their bodies in the usual horrible fashion.   Nobody was spared, man, woman, or child, that I could see. The Chinese appeared to offer no resistance.   Many of them prostrated themselves on the ground before the butchers with abject submission, and were shot or stabbed in that posture.

I was now to have a close shave.   I came suddenly and unawares upon a party engaged in slaughtering some shrieking wretches—women and children amongst them—and being perceived was shot at by one of the soldiers. I rapidly retreated, but he detached himself in pursuit. I entered a house; he followed, but I had the start of him, and for a while evaded him. I got into what looked like a kitchen or scullery, and amongst some other utensils I came upon a curiously shaped hatchet, very heavy and sharp. I waited for about a quarter of an hour, and then, judging that the Jap must have left when unable to find me, I prepared to sally forth again, as it was rather more dangerous to be in the houses than in the streets, the soldiers entering and pillaging them one by one, and of course slaughtering anybody they found within. No sooner, however, had I got to the front, than I unexpectedly encountered the very man who had driven me in, retiring laden with booty. He dropped his plunder at once upon seeing me, and handled his bayonet to run me through. We were in a little low room, with a door in a corner opening on the street. He made a furious thrust at me; by a quick movement I evaded it. The steel grazed my left side, and crashed through the wall behind me, to which I was pinned by the clothes, and as he tried to withdraw his weapon, I had a fair stroke at him in return. The axe was very sharp; rage and

G

despair seemed to have doubled my strength, and I split his skull half-way down to the jaw. Brains and blood were scattered over me, as he sank dead at my feet.

I felt no inclination to stay any longer, and was about to take my departure, when it struck me that I might as well arm myself with my defunct antagonist's rifle and cartridge-pouch. This led immediately to a better idea. The Jap was a man of nearly my own stature; why not put on his clothes? It was fast darkening, and aided in the deception by the obscurity, my chance of escape would be greatly increased, though I began to have an uneasy feeling that it would be a miracle if I escaped destruction anyhow. I immediately acted on the inspiration. The soldier, I have said, was nearly of my own height (5 ft. 6 in.), but I was a good deal broader across the shoulders, and I made an extensive split up the back of his tunic in struggling into it. That, however, was no great matter, and I was soon equipped in all his outer casement, except his cap, which had been bisected along with his head. There was a little keen dagger in his belt, and with it I cut off my moustache as close as I could, as the Japanese seldom have much hair on their faces. Then, not forgetting his rifle, a beautiful Lee-Metford, I sallied forth, carrying my discarded clothes over my arm, a circumstance not at all likely to attract attention, as they were all loading themselves with booty.

I was undecided enough how to proceed. I might pass out into the open country north of the town, but if I did so I should probably either die of starvation or get killed as a Japanese straggler. I began to think my best course would be to return to the port, and take my chance of getting away in some small vessel. First of all, however, I resolved to complete my intention of seeing what was going on at the inn, to which I was now quite close. I kept boldly on, and my disguise answered admirably, not one of the soldiers seeming to suspect that I was anything but a comrade. Now and then I would be greeted by wild cries in their high, shrill voices, or one, waving his rifle, would shout something as he passed. I returned the greetings in dumb show, and hurried on. I do not know how it would have fared with me in broad daylight; probably not nearly so well; but it was now nearly dark. Most of the soldiers had provided themselves, to light the work of slaughter and pillage, with one of those coloured lanterns which are to be found in such profusion in Chinese towns, and their demoniac aspect was greatly heightened by the illuminations they carried as they flitted to and fro. The butchery was pro-

ceeding without the least sign of abatement; shots,
shouts, shrieks, and groans resounded on every
side; the streets presented a fearful spectacle; the
ground was saturated with blood, and everywhere
strewn with horribly mutilated corpses; some of
the narrower avenues were positively choked with
carnage.   The dead were mostly the townspeople;
their valiant defenders seemed to have been able
to make themselves scarce; where they all got to
is a mystery to me; perhaps owing to the fact that
they got rid of their uniforms early in the proceedings in order not to be identified as com-
batants, a dodge that must have served them very
little, as the conquerors killed every one they came
across.

At length I reached Sen's house, only to find
that the destroyer had been there.   The place was
in darkness; I took down the lantern from over
the outer gate, with the name of the inn and its
proprietor's written on it in the Chinese character,
lit it, and began an inspection.   The first thing I
saw was the corpse of my landlord himself, lying
in the covered court. His head was almost severed,
and he had been disembowelled.   Most of the
lower storey rooms had doors opening into this
court; across the threshold of one lay the corpse
of a female servant, mutilated in an unspeakable
manner.   The household establishment consisted

in all of some ten or twelve persons, and eight of
them I found lying murdered in different parts of
the premises.   There was no sign of living presence anywhere.   The place had been thoroughly
ransacked, and everything worth having carried
off.   My blood boiled as I surveyed the scene of
desolation and massacre, where lately I had witnessed happiness and cheerful industry, and I felt
that I could willingly have died myself on the spot
to obtain vengeance on the murderers.

In one of the upper rooms there was a bamboo
ladder and trap leading on the roof, which was flat,
and it occurred to me to ascend and look round.
It was quite dark, and there was little to be seen
beyond the limits of the street.   Distant illuminations marked the positions of the forts on the surrounding heights.   The seaward ones were still in
possession of the Chinese.   They fell easily on the
following day, and had been practically abandoned.
I noticed that the sounds of violence in the town
were rapidly decreasing.   As I walked slowly
round, the dim light of my lantern fell on two
figures skulking in the shadow.   They retreated as
I advanced, until they could back no further, and
then one of them fell on his knees before me, bow-
ing his forehead on the roof with abject cries.   I
held the lantern towards him, and to my astonish-
ment recognized Chung.   He evidently did not

know me, and no wonder, considering the manner in which I had rigged myself out. He seemed half out of his wits with fear, and I had some difficulty in forcing the fact of my identity upon his conviction. Then his delight was as great as his previous terror. His companion was a stranger to him—a man of exceedingly gentlemanly and prepossessing appearance, and clearly a person of condition, being, in fact, as I afterwards found, a mandarin. His own residence had been sacked and his family murdered. He and a brother had escaped into the street, were pursued, and his relative shot in running away. Though with his left arm broken by a bullet, he had run into the inn. When the soldiers entered it he and Chung got on to the roof, where none of the Japanese thought of looking for victims. His broken arm was causing him considerable suffering, and having acquired during my knock-about life some rude knowledge of surgery, I put the fracture together, and made a sling with my neck-tie.

I explained my situation to Chung as well as I was able; he translated to his countryman, who knew no English, and we held a council as to future proceedings. The work of slaughter had apparently been suspended; either the soldiers were tired of it or had been recalled. The Japanese forces exceeded 20,000, and of these I do not think that more than one half, perhaps not one third, were engaged in this first evening's work, which was only the opening scene of the massacre. Masses of the troops had been placed to occupy the forts, and otherwise secure the conquest. We thought it likely, as indeed was the case, that they would all withdraw to the camps outside as the night advanced, and we resolved to attempt to gain the water-side, and seek a last chance of escape, under cover of darkness. We searched the place for food, but all we could find was a little bread, and a few prepared sweetmeat cakes.

An awful stillness, broken at times by ominous sounds, came over the town. Lights flitted at times through its dark labyrinths, by whom borne it was impossible to perceive. The presence of death, in its most fearful shapes, seemed palpable to the senses, and we, crouching in the gloom on the roof, to which as the safest place we had returned, had before our mental vision the mutilated bodies in the rooms close below us, with the ghastly probability, almost the certainty, that another hour or two would join us in their horrid fate. To myself, the reckless, wasted past presented itself, in that situation of appalling terrors, in all its enormity. There was I, after throwing away the high advantages of fortune and prosperity, a ruined and degraded man, about to meet an appropriate ending to such a career by a bloody death at the hands of some brutal soldier, in an unknown land, at the ends of the earth, where scarcely a human being knew a word of my native tongue. If these pages should be read by any young man embarking without a thought of the future, in the flush of high spirits and inexperience, upon courses similar to mine, I hope he will take warning, and stop in time.

It was, I should judge, about ten o'clock when at last we descended to the street. There had been no firing for about two hours. The lantern was re-lit, and Chung, who knew the way best, took it and went ahead. I still wore the soldier's dress ; if met and challenged, I proposed to make it appear, as best I could, that I was making the Chinamen conduct me to one of the camps, or if I failed in this to sell my life dearly with the rifle.

Our path lay right across the town, and the dead lay thickly in nearly every street in the quarters we traversed, where, of every age, sex, and condition, they had been promiscuously butchered by the hundred. Here and there the miserable survivors —survivors only for the present—were searching, with low wailings and lamentations, for those they had lost, with the aid of their coloured lanterns, which gave a look of indescribable ghastliness to the mutilated forms they bent over to examine.

To my last day I shall remember, with unfading
horror, the aspect of those remnants of mortality, in
all the hideousness stamped upon them by the un-
namable atrocities practised during that diabolical
orgy of murder and mutilation, rape, lust, and
rapine. This is war! Away, in the splendid
pavilion of the vanquished, the conquering marshal,
surrounded by his generals and officers, was in-
stalled in triumph, secure of his country's applause
and his emperor's favour; but here, amid these
desolated homes, these mutilated heaps of death,
was the night side, the shadow, of their glory.
And this was but the first day of *four!* It must
be admitted that the Chinese drew it upon themselves, that everywhere else the Japanese behaved
with admirable clemency and moderation; but after
making every allowance, their conduct in this
instance, and particularly that of the high commanding chiefs in never seeking to put a stop to the
devilish excesses perpetrated before their eyes on
unoffending non-combatants, is richly deserving of
everlasting infamy.

Many of the poor wretches thus cowering about
ran away upon perceiving, as they thought, an
armed Japanese soldier, but in one instance I had
reason to be thankful that I was not alone. A
middle-aged man and two younger ones were carrying away, in one of the streets we traversed, the

half-naked body of a woman, which had been split
open from the abdomen to the chest. The elder
man glared upon me, in the dim light, with the
expression of a tiger, and drawing a long curved
knife from his breast, and pointing at me, shouted
something to his companions, who perhaps were
his sons. Chung at once interposed, and talked
with them rapidly for a few moments, and naturally
his explanation sufficed and we proceeded. I asked
Chung what the man had said :—" There is one of
the Japanese devils; let us rip him up."

But it would only be needlessly harrowing to
dwell on the sights of horror we encountered at
every turn. We pressed on, rapidly yet cautiously,
our feet dabbling in blood wherever we trod. As
we proceeded down a street about ten feet broad,
we heard in front sounds as of voices shouting and
singing. The avenue we were in took a turn about
fifteen yards in advance of us, and as we hesitated
and finally stopped, there appeared round it a body
of men in whom we at once recognized the Japanese
soldiers. There was a low but wide doorway on
our right, and into it we at once slipped with no
trifling celerity. It was intensely dark and offered
a good concealment. We could not afford to ex-
tinguish our lantern, and I placed it behind an
angle of the inner wall where it was impossible that
its glimmer could be seen from the street. Crouch-

ing in the deep shadow, we anxiously awaited the passing of the soldiers, whose voices we heard momentarily approaching, shouting at their full pitch a discordant song, accompanied by a loud ringing sound which at first I mistook for that of some instrument. They were soon abreast of us, some twenty or thirty in number. I scarcely breathed as the ferocious band went trooping past. Their appearance was ghastly and terrible beyond conception. They were literally recking from the shambles of inhuman butchery; their clothes and weapons were smeared and clotted with blood; some held human heads aloft on their bayonets; the lanterns which most of them carried, and swung to and fro as they marched, threw on their repulsive figures and savage Oriental faces, their white teeth, oblique eyes, and sallow countenances, a weird, wavering light, appropriate to their infernal aspect; they looked more like demons than like men. The foremost, who appeared to be dismounted dragoons, were clashing their sabres together in a kind of accompaniment to the yelling chant in which they all joined. On they went, trampling the dead with whom their bestial ferocity had strewn the devoted town, the sound of their high shrill voices and the ring of the clashing steel being audible for some time after they had passed out of sight. At length it died away and all was still again, so silent that

I seemed to hear the quick and heavy throbbing of my heart.

After waiting two or three minutes I told Chung to take the lantern so that we might set out again. He did so, but as he was about to step from the doorway he tripped over some object concealed by the darkness and fell: it was a dead body. I examined it by the lantern-light. There were several deep bayonet wounds and a terrific sabre-slash across the face which had completely destroyed the left eye. The abdomen was abominably mutilated. A knife was clenched in the right hand of the victim, showing that he had not died without an effort to defend himself. I swung the lantern about the recess, and perceived further back three or four steps, ascending to a door slightly open. These steps were covered with blood which seemed to flow from behind the door. I pushed it open, and entered the place to which it gave access. It seemed to be a kind of public office—a wide, low, bare apartment, divided on one side by a massive wooden counter, surmounted by a partition pierced at intervals with pigeon-holes, as if for communication between persons on opposite sides of the division. It may have been a bank or money-changer's office. It is not, however, on account of the place itself, but of its contents, that I describe it. The floor was covered with the corpses of men, women, and children, mingled indiscriminately together, fugitives who had there taken refuge and been relentlessly butchered. The bodies had been decapitated, and the bloody heads stuck up on a long row of spikes which surmounted the wooden partition over the counter. Both Chung and the mandarin uttered a cry of terror as we caught sight of those distorted countenances, grinning upon us with the livid stare of violent death through the dim medium of the coloured lamplight. My blood seemed to freeze as my eyes encountered that ghastly gaze of the dead, to which the upright position of the heads gave a sort of semblance or mockery of life. An infant a few months old was pinned to the counter below by a sharp piece of iron run through its little body. The floor was two or three inches deep in thickening blood and the entrails of the mutilated bodies. The arms and legs as well as heads had been hacked off some of them and flung about the place. Altogether a more hideous and revolting spectacle than this chamber of horrors can never have been presented to mortal gaze. Such a scene, and the sickening smell of blood, drove us out again almost immediately. At that moment another party of the Japanese passed our hiding-place. An infantry soldier in advance carried a large uncovered flambeau, which threw a broad, red, steady glare over

all surrounding objects. I at once saw that these
were all officers, excepting two or three; smart,
well-got-up, gentlemanly-looking little men in the
extreme; returning, perhaps, from calling off the
last of their bloody war-dogs, or making sure that
all resistance had ceased. They were laughing and
chatting gaily, as if the massacre were rather a
pleasant affair than otherwise. When they had
gone by, we issued into the street, but had proceeded only a few paces when we saw a man carrying a lantern appear round the abrupt bend before
mentioned. He looked like another Japanese
hurrying after his companions who had just passed.
We returned with all haste to the doorway; and as
we judged that he had probably seen us, we re-
entered the inner slaughter-house and closed the
door. We were right in thinking we had been
seen, and in about a minute we heard steps outside
the door, which was presently thrust violently open
and the soldier entered, a low, sinister figure, holding a drawn sword in what seemed to me a curiously
white hand. He peered into the obscurity, perceived me, and doubtless taking me, in the uncertain light, for a Japanese, from the clothes I wore,
lowered his weapon and addressed me in a harsh
authoritative tone. The sound of the language
was singularly like that of Italian. He pointed to
the Chinamen, probably asking what they were. I

took advantage of his unguarded pause to plunge
my bayonet in his body, with a thrust so rapid that
he had not time to make the least movement to
avoid it. He fell at once where he stood, but
attempted to rise again, when I gave him another
prick which settled his business. He fell back
heavily against the counter with a groan. One of
the heads above was shaken off its spike by the
concussion and struck him on the shoulder as he
lay. His eyes, opening and shutting convulsively,
seemed to gaze upon the ghastly object. He
groaned again, and in a few moments was dead. I
bent over him with the lantern, and soon perceived
from the richness of his uniform and accoutrements,
as well as from the look of caste about the head
and face, that I had killed an officer of high rank.
He wore white gloves, which accounted for the odd
look of his hands when he appeared on the threshold. I felt sorry when I realized that he was a
man of consequence and authority, for had I perceived it at first I would certainly have endea-
voured to obtain his protection for myself and my
companions; but Chung had slunk behind me with
the lantern, the officer's own was a very dim one,
so that in the obscurity I could only make out that
he was a Japanese soldier, and expecting to be
attacked judged it prudent to get my blow in first.
Having given him what his countrymen called the

"happy despatch," he could be of no further use to us. Before again leaving the place, I took possession of his sword, which was a very beautiful and valuable weapon, the hilt ornamented by a quantity of massive and richly-chased gold, and a great number of tiny diamonds and rubies,—infinitesimal gems, set in pretty, quaint devices, with a larger stone here and there. This trophy I brought away with me from Port Arthur, but when in Liverpool at the beginning of the year of grace 1896, the pressure of financial exigency compelled me to entrust it to the temporary care of the universal uncle of mankind, who said it was worth £600 or £700. I could by no means persuade him to believe my account of how it came into my possession. He laughed and said I was making fun of him. His obstinate incredulity was amusing. "You're a sailor, sir, I see," he said, "and we know what sailors' yarns are in this town. I've heard a few of them."

Again stealing outside, we resumed our perilous way through this city of dreadful night. We lost no time in turning out of the street where had occurred the incidents just described, and which seemed in the track of stragglers moving towards the adjacent Golden Hill fort. We left it by a very narrow lane abutting at right angles. The other end of this was blocked by a heap of corpses which we had to climb over. As I was doing so a hideous groan struck my ear, and the body under my foot seemed to heave. I started back, and simultaneously the apparent corpse rose up, a tall, blood-besmeared figure, which stared horribly upon me for a moment and then, with another loud and horrid groan, fell prone on his back, his arms widely extended. I lost no time in scrambling past him after my companions, who had run away, and small blame to them, for it was like the rising of a corpse suddenly endowed with volition. Both were by this time in what has been forcibly and picturesquely described as a " blue funk "; they trembled ceaselessly; their teeth chattered, and their eyes roved here and there with a wild, hunted look; every now and then they stopped convulsively, imagining that they saw or heard something to indicate the proximity of the ferocious murderers. As for myself, if my outward man were less open to reproach, my inward condition was nothing much to boast of, and truly the horrors which continually presented themselves, joined to the oppressive midnight shadow and stillness which hung over the place of doom, would have damaged the nerve of a football referee.

We reached the basin through a series of open brick-works, used as timber stores, on its north side. Everything was darkness and desertion.

H

The moon was rising far beyond the West Port
away in our front, but it was in the last quarter
and afforded little light.   There were very few stars
visible.   The night had turned piercingly cold, but
so great was my mental anxiety and excitement
that I seemed unaffected in body by the severity of
the weather.   With the lantern we began to search
about for a boat, at first without success.   In a
square-shaped inlet or creek a little above the dockyard we presently came upon another horrifying
spectacle.   A junk lay stranded in the shallows.
It was literally full of dead bodies, and many lay
on the adjacent shore.   The unfortunates had
evidently been pursued down to where the junk
lay, and slaughtered before they could get it off.
It struck me that what we were looking for, a boat,
might in all probability be found on board the fatal
vessel.   It lay heeled over broadside to the beach,
and I waded out to it through the shallow water.
I gained the upper deck with some difficulty and
stood amidst the mass of carnage.   Rifle-balls had
done the work of death.   Many of the bodies were
in army uniforms.   I could find only two boats.
One, a mere cockle-shell, had been perforated by
bullets and rendered useless.   Another lay inboard
on the quarter-deck, but it was so filled and covered
with corpses that at first I did not notice it.   It
seemed in fair condition, but the task of ridding it

of its horrible freight was so repugnant that I
returned on shore to resume the search for one
elsewhere. It was in vain, however; all we could
find in the vicinity was an old sampan, which
besides being very leaky, was more than three men
could manage, only one of them, moreover, having
any knowledge of sailoring. There was nothing
for it but to return to the death-ship. We all went
on board this time, and applied ourselves to the
work. The pile of dead were dragged away, and
with considerable labour, and aided by the careened
condition of the junk, we managed to launch the
boat, which had been secured inside the bulwark.
It was in a horrid state with blood, but we were
not in a situation to be particular. We found a
quantity of provisions and fresh water—or rather
water which had once been fresh—in the cook-
house of the junk.

It must have been after midnight when we
shoved off and got afloat. Neither of my companions were experts with an oar, and could render
me very little aid; moreover, Chinese oars, like
Chinese belongings altogether, are very unlike anything else in the world and need some practice to
use. We were, however, close to the entrance of
the port, which being defended by torpedoes and
mines, we ran little risk of encountering Japanese
vessels, although the submarine dangers threatened

us as well, if we strayed from the deep-water channel in the dark. We got on in safety, though very slowly, and another two hours had been consumed before we were through.

What to do next I had no fixed idea. One thing, however, was assured, that it was certain death to stay in Port Arthur, and that our only chance, slender as it seemed at best, consisted in getting as far away as possible. I resolved, after some consideration, to hold on south round the extremity of the Peninsula.

In the seaward forts above us we could discern no signs of activity, and only a light here and there, far out on the misty expanse of waters, showed the position of the Japanese war-vessels, which had an easy job of it as far as Port Arthur was concerned. The weather, though so bitterly cold, was far from stormy, yet the difficulty of rowing was increased naturally when we got out into the heavier waters of the sea. So unpromising in fact did our situation look, that I began to reflect whether it would not be better to stay about the mouth of the harbour, and allow ourselves to be taken by some Japanese ship, than wander off I knew not where, probably in the end to perish of starvation. Luck decided the point. We had painfully made a couple of miles from the estuary of the harbour, when we came upon a large junk stranded on a sand-bank. There were no lights showing on board her; in the obscurity we could see nobody; yet she did not look like a wreck, and at first we did not know what to make of it. After a consultation, it was decided to fire a shot from the rifle and see what it would lead to. No sooner had the report rung out, than there was a bustle and stir on the vessel's decks, which appeared suddenly to swarm with men, and became illuminated by lanterns. I told Chung to hail. He did so, and a voice replied in Chinese. We drew close abreast, and my companions held a parley with those on board. Our situation explained we were permitted to ascend. The junk was full of men. She had got into her present predicament in escaping, and they were waiting for the morning flood tide to float her off. Two or three junks, we were told, had struck torpedoes in leaving the harbour and been blown in pieces, and many others had fallen into the clutches of the enemy. Those on board, besides her usual crew, were chiefly soldiers. With the profound deference paid to rank by the Orientals, the chief cabin was at once given up to the mandarin, who insisted on my sharing it with him. He and Chung gave a most glowing account of me to those on board, to whom, in my remarkable accoutrement, I was an object of legitimate curiosity.

Exhausted by exertion and anxiety, I was fast

asleep within half-an-hour after stepping up the junk's side. I slept far into the day, and when I emerged found that she had been successfully floated off the bank, and got out to sea without so far attracting the notice of the Japanese ships.

CHAPTER VII

A VERY queer craft is a Chinese junk. Few
Europeans have any defined idea what they are
like. They are of different sizes, most of them
suited to the numerous rivers and canals which
intersect the country in every part. The largest
are of about one thousand tons burden. The whole
mode of building is most peculiar. Instead of the
timbers being first raised as with us, they are the
last in their places, and the vessel is put together
with immense spiked nails. The next process is
doubling and clamping above and below decks.
Two immense beams or string pieces are then
ranged below, fore and aft, and keep the other
beams in their places. The deck-frames are an
arch, and a platform erected on it protects it from
the sun, and from other injuries otherwise inevit-
able. The seams are caulked either with old
fishing-net or bamboo shavings, and then paid
with a cement called chinam, consisting of oyster-
shells burnt to lime, with a mixture of fine bamboo

shavings, pounded together with a vegetable oil extracted from a ground nut. When dried it becomes excessively hard; it never starts, and the seams thus secured are perfectly safe and watertight. All the work about her is of the roughest kind. The trees when found of a suitable size are cut down, stripped of their bark, and sawn into convenient lengths; the sides are not squared, but left just as they grew. No artificial means are resorted to for any bends; a tree or branch of a tree is found with the requisite natural curvature. There is not in the building, rigging, or fitting-up of a Chinese junk one single thing which is similar to what we see on board a European vessel. Everything is different; the mode of construction; the absence of keel, bowsprit, and shrouds; the materials employed; the mast, the sails, the yard, the rudder, the compass, the anchor—all are dissimilar.

The vessel in which I now found myself, the *King-Shing*, was of about seven hundred tons. She was built entirely of teak, and her skipper, or Ty Kong, as he is called, alleged that she was more than a hundred years old, and said that one of her crew who had recently died, had served in her for fifty years. Her extreme length was one hundred and sixty feet; breadth of beam, twenty-five feet and a half; depth of hold, twelve feet;

height of poop from the water, thirty-eight feet; height of bow, thirty feet. Her most attractive portion was the saloon, or state cabin, the beauty of whose furniture and decorations formed a curious contrast to the rude and rough workmanship of the cabin itself. Its carved and gilded entrance was protected by a sort of skylight, the sides of which were formed of the prepared oyster-shells so commonly used in China instead of glass, the latter being too expensive for general purposes. The enclosure was thirty feet long, twenty-five broad, and eleven in height. From the beams overhead were suspended numbers of the different kinds of lanterns used in China. They were of every imaginable form, size, and variety of material. The sides and deck-roof were of a yellow ground, and covered with paintings of flowers, leaves, fruit, insects, birds, monkeys, dogs, and cats; some of those latter animals were what in heraldic language would be called *queue-fourchée*. The place was filled with a vast assortment of curious and beautiful articles, gathered together during the long existence of the vessel. To give a list of them would require pages; brought to Europe they would have made the reputations of a dozen museums.

At the end of the saloon was the Joss-house, or idol-house, containing the idol Chin-Tee, having eighteen arms, with her attendants, Tung-Sam and

Tung-See. The richly-gilt idol was made of one solid piece of camphor-wood, and had a red scarf thrown round it. An altar-table, also of camphor-wood, and painted red, stood in front of the Joss-house, with an incense burner placed upon it. The red ground of the table had gilt carvings of flowers and insects, and the imperial dragons with the ball of flame between them. On each side of the front was a square place painted green, with words in Chinese inviting worshippers to bring gold and agate stones as offerings.

The sleeping berths of the crew were all *aft*, on a lower deck. Close by these was the most astonishing part of the vessel, the colossal rudder, not hung with pintles and gudgeons, the vessel having no stern-post, but suspended to two windlasses by three large ropes made of cane and hemp; one round a windlass on the next deck, and two round a windlass on the upper deck of all, so that it could be raised or lowered according to the depth of water. When lowered to its full extent it drew about twenty-four feet, being twelve feet more than the draught of the vessel. It was steered on this berth-deck when fully lowered. It was also drawn close into the stern, into a kind of socket, by means of two immense bamboo ropes attached to the bottom of the rudder, passing beneath the bottom of the vessel, and coming over the bow on the upper deck, and there hove in taut and fastened. When let down to its greatest depth it required occasionally the strength of fifteen men to move the large tiller.

On ascending to the next deck, one passed under a covering made of oyster-shells, similar to that over the entrance to the saloon; under this hung a flag which had been borne before the Emperor on one of the most solemn religious processions. On a piece of wood near one of the windlasses was inscribed—"May the sea never wash over this junk." Close by was the sailors' Joss-house, containing the deity of the sea with her two attendants, each with a red scarf. Near the principal goddess was a piece of the wood from the first timber of the junk that was laid; this was taken to one of their principal temples, there consecrated, and then brought on board, and placed as symbolic of the whole vessel's being under the protection of the deity. A small earthen pot, containing sacred earth and rice, stood in front, in which Joss-sticks and other incense was burnt. A lighted lamp, too, was here always kept burning; if it had gone out during a voyage it would have been considered an omen of bad luck. On the right and left, before coming to this Joss-house, were paintings. One panel represented the Mandarin Ducks; another, a Chinese lady at her toilette; a third, a globe of gold-fish.   On this deck were cabins for passengers and supercargoes, the doors painted with different devices.   Above was the lofty poop-deck, with one of the rudder-windlasses on it, and the mizzen-mast, fifty feet long, and placed on one side, in order to allow the tiller to work when in shallow water.   The main-mast was ninety-five feet in length, and ten feet in circumference at the bottom.   It was one spar of teak, and just as the tree grew with merely the bark taken off.   It was not perfectly straight —a defect with us, but not so considered by the Chinese, who prefer a mast with a bend in it to one without, thinking it adds to the strength, and is conclusive evidence of the goodness of the spar. This mast was hooped round, in consequence of being cracked while undergoing the process of hardening.   The mode adopted for this purpose by the Chinese is to bury the timber for a con-siderable time in marshy ground; thus treated, they say teak becomes hard as iron.   The mast did not go within four feet of the bottom—the ship having no kelson—but, to use the technical term, was "toggled" to two large pieces of wood which answered as partners.   To these were added two other heavy pieces as chocks, which were intended to keep the huge spars in their places.   Neither stays nor shrouds were used.   The main yards were made of teak quite rough; the upper one was seventy-five feet long, and the lower sixty.

The sails were made of closely-woven matting, a substance much lighter than canvas. It holds the wind better, and rarely splits, because it never shakes in the wind. So large and heavy was the mainsail of the *King-Shing*, that it required forty men with the aid of the capstan to raise it. Without the capstan eighty men would have been needed. It had eighteen reefs. The sails were reefed by being lowered, which precluded any necessity for going aloft.

The vane was in the shape of a fish, the body formed of rattan work, the head and gills of painted matting, with two projections like the antennæ of a butterfly. The tail was furnished with long streamers, and little flags were stuck in the body for additional ornament. There were also Chinese characters painted on the body signifying "Good luck to the Junk." Between the main-mast and fore-mast were two large rough windlasses stretching across the deck, and used for getting up the anchor. By the entrance to the forecastle were two water-tanks, capable of holding one thousand five hundred gallons each. The fore-mast was seventy-five feet from the deck. It raked forward, and was supported by a large piece of wood on the after part, and secured similarly to the main-mast. The anchors were of wood, the flukes shod with iron, and attached to the shank by strong lashings of bamboo. The stock was composed of three separate pieces of wood lashed together by rattan ropes, and was fixed to the crown. As the Chinese drag their anchors on board instead of catting and fishing as other seamen do, this position of the stock offers no impediment. The flukes were of the same dimensions as those of similar sized anchors with us; they were straight and not rounded, and there were no palms. There was also a kedge, with only one fluke. The cables were of rattan. The junk had no bitts, but to supply their place the strong beams across the deck had large holes for stoppers. The " wales " formed another singular feature of the vessel—airtight boxes, projecting three feet from the side; their object was to make the vessel more buoyant, to enable her to carry more cargo, and prevent her rolling, but this last, in my opinion, was chiefly prevented by the size and position of the rudder.

The cook-house was placed differently from the galleys of European vessels, being aft of the mainmast. The lower part was built of brick, with two square holes in front for the fires. Troughs of water were placed in front of these holes, so that any ignited fuel that might drop out would be at once extinguished. Wood was the fuel used. For

cooking they used iron pans surrounded by red
tiles. One was covered by a kind of half cask;
this was used for boiling the rice, the cover being
to preserve the steam after the water was boiled
away, which causes the rice to be beautifully done
and not soddened, as is often the case in our cooking. It also prevents it from being thrown out
when the vessel rolls. The quantity of rice for
each man was about three pounds daily. All
washing of dishes, etc., was performed on a stage
outside the galley so that it might be kept perfectly
clean. The proper allowance for each mess was
delivered in front. Close to the cook-house was a
water-tank of wood, painted in imitation of bricks,
and capable of holding three thousand gallons.

Such was the *King-Shing* junk, and such are
most of the craft of the Celestials. They would
appear to be gradually coming round to Western
ideas in the matter of ships, and in fact have done
so entirely for war purposes, but the fashions of
their ancestors are still good enough for most of
them, and the junk is to be seen everywhere. Not
a mere thing of yesterday is the junk. Vessels
essentially similar to the one I have described were
navigating the Chinese seas and rivers when the
fleets of Rome and Carthage were contesting the
supremacy of the Mediterranean, and long before.
Rome and Carthage, and many another mighty

maritime power, have risen and passed away utterly, like bubbles, or dreams, but the Chinaman and his everlasting junk are still here.

The vessel belonged to some mandarins at Shanghai, who used it for trading to Cochin-China. It had recently, however, been despatched with a cargo to Cheefoo, had been blown away north by a gale, and forced to run into the harbour at Port Arthur to escape the Japanese. There it had lain until the place fell. The crew numbered fifty-four, all told.

After floating off the sand-bank, and getting an offing, we were within the Gulf of Pechili, and determined to make for one or other of its ports, but on the first day we encountered a very heavy nor'-wester, which blew us far out of the Gulf. When, after lasting a day and a night, the gale abated, we were well down the Yellow Sea, and the skipper, or Ty Kong, whose name was Sam-Sing, determined to hold on for the port where the junk's owners dwelt. I had no objection to make to this, nor had the mandarin, who possessed friends and relatives in the south. The soldiers on board, however, were very discontented and mutinous, and as they considerably outnumbered the crew I began to fear trouble. They were all from northern provinces and had no desire to go south. Their language was scarcely intelligible even to their nominal countrymen. The immense diversity of dialects in China is, in fact, a great hindrance to progress by preventing the unification of the people. After some excited discussion they were prevailed upon to acquiesce by the solemn promise of the mandarin to make arrangements with the authorities for their return to their own parts, or failing that to send them back at his own expense; besides, the representation that to turn north again would most likely end in capture by the Japanese vessels, through whose present cruising-ground the gale had luckily blown us, had great weight.

I was vastly amused, during my voyage in the *King-Shing*, by the superstitions of her crew. Their devotion to their idols was indeed truly edifying. A religious man, according to his lights, was Sam-Sing, and rigidly punctual in the daily observance of incense-burning, gong-banging, and other rites supposed to be propitiatory of the deity. He was also, however, greatly addicted to opium-smoking, and when under the influence of the drug, of which, as an old stager, he could consume great quantities without being stupefied, the idea of the occult power of the goddess, never absent from his mind, was turned completely upside down. When free from the fumes of opium nobody could have been more respectful to the Josses, but when intoxicated, and with the weather threatening, he

I

openly poured upon them abuse, reviling, and
suspicion. He usually started a pipe of opium
about noon, and the change in his demeanour came
round gradually during the afternoon. In the
morning he was sober and pious, in the evening
intoxicated and blasphemous, particularly, as I
have said, when the weather was bad. "As for
that infernal Chin-Tee," he would say in effect,
shaking his fist in the direction of the idol, "it's all
her fault we're in this mess. What's the use of her
—lazy harridan! Much she cares what becomes
of us"—and so on till overpowered by excess.
When by the next morning he had slept off his
debauch, and came round to recollection of his
enormities, his penitence knew no bounds; he
would prostrate himself in the Joss-house, and in
the most abject terms implore forgiveness for his
intemperate language over-night. Then he would
generally abstain for two or three days, but at the
first sign of bad weather, he took to his pipe, and
Chin-Tee came in for another blast of abuse. The
rest of the crew were always horrified by the shocking impiety of the Ty Kong, and on more than one
occasion I really feared that they were about to
proceed to Jonahize him. They were by no means
all opium-smokers; some of them smoked tobacco,
of a vile quality, in metal pipes, with an under-
hanging curved portion containing water, through

which the smoke passed. The opium-pipe is a quite different thing. It is a reed of about an inch in diameter, and the aperture in the bowl for the admission of the opium is not larger than a pin's head. The drug is prepared by boiling and evaporation to the consistence of treacle. Very few whiffs can be taken from a single pipe, but one is enough to have an effect on a beginner, as I have already described in my own case, but an old hand, like the Ty Kong, can smoke for hours.

The incense burned before the idols consisted mostly of pieces of aromatic wood, called Joss-sticks, silvered paper, and tin-foil. One of their most revered objects was the mariner's compass, and before it they would place tea, sweet cake, and pork, in order to keep it faithful and true! It is well known that the Chinese were acquainted with the phenomenon of the magnetized needle centuries before it was known in Europe, and their compass differs materially from ours; instead of consisting of a movable card attached to the needle, theirs is simply a needle of little more than an inch in length balanced in a glazed hole in the centre of a solid wooden dish, finely varnished. It has only twenty-four points, and with its use they combine some of their most ancient astrological ideas. The broad circumference of the dish is marked off into concentric circles, inscribed with mystical figures.

We say the needle points to the north; they hold
that the attraction is to the south, and therefore
colour that end of the needle red, a hue that ap-
pears to have a mysterious efficacy in their eyes.
I have already told how the Josses were wrapped
in red scarves, and bits of red cloth were tied on
the rudder, cable, mast, and other principal parts
of the vessel, as safeguards against danger.   There
was also a large painted eye on either side of the
bow, to enable the junk to see her way!   At first I
could not understand the meaning of this, and told
Chung to ask the Ty Kong for an explanation.
" Have eye," translated Chung, " can see; no have
eye, no can see."   On occasions of special religious
demonstration these optics were decorated with
strips of red cloth.   On one occasion when a
steamer suspiciously like a Japanese cruiser hove
in sight, they tied red rags to their antique guns,
or gin-galls, and with this consecration on their
defensive arrangements, seemed to feel perfectly
secure.   I suppose the English-trained crews of
their navy must have been persuaded out of these
amazing notions, and taught the European compass, but the ideas of Sam-Sing and his merry men
were as old as their vessel.

I have not yet described my mandarin friend.
His name was Ki-Chang; he was a mandarin of
the fifth class, his distinctive mark being a crystal

button on the top of his cap. He was forty-six years old, intelligent, amiable, and gentlemanly. He and I had much intercourse during the voyage, with Chung for an interpreter. I taught him a little English, and how to write his name in English, an accomplishment of which he seemed extremely proud. Like most of the educated Chinese, he wrote his own language very beautifully. He was a wealthy and influential man.

The *King-Shing* showed herself a remarkably good sea-boat, but desperately slow. No device could get more than eight knots out of her, and this was much above her average. We encountered one or two violent storms, in which she behaved wonderfully. One night the wind, after veering all round the compass with vivid lightning and thunder, settled in the south-west and blew a perfect hurricane. All sails were lowered, except half the foresail, and twenty-five men were required at the mammoth rudder. We were obliged to start some eight tons of water out of the deck tanks, and everything on deck, fore and aft, was secured. The junk laboured heavily, but shipped no water. At daybreak the weather moderated, and we were able to set more sail; but in two or three hours the wind chopped round to the north-west, and blew more fiercely than ever, attended by squalls of hailstones as big as marbles, the knocks of which made my countenance look as if I had come off second-best in a middle-weight "scrap." We lowered the main-sail again, and set four reefs of fore-sail to scud under. At three o'clock the vessel took a tremendous lurch, and washed away our lee-quarter boat. It was dark, and the sea barely discernible at a distance of thirty yards, being blown into a thick mist. At six the hurricane continued with unabated fury with terrific squalls; a fearful sea struck the ship and nearly broached her to. The sea was a mass of foam, and running very high, but kept down to some extent by the violence of the wind. Later we were running under bare poles. Again the gale went down, and again we got up sail, but without warning a tremendous squall struck us and laid us on our beam ends. A boat was blown away, the foresail split, and through the carelessness of the men at the rudder they jibed the mainsail; it came over with terrific force, but fortunately did no harm. Luckily the sails could be very easily and rapidly lowered. One only had to let go or cut the halyards and down they came. Throughout all this the junk behaved in a manner which astounded me. She actually never shipped any water, that which came aboard being tops of seas blown off. But the very qualities which made her so steady-going militated against her speed.

She was a safe boat at all points. One night we had to anchor off a dead lee-shore; the crew decorated their cables with some extra red rags, and with death grinning under our lee, went to supper with a serenity which I should have been glad to be able to imitate. But their confidence was as well grounded as their anchors, which held with an unshakable tenacity.

Though so long acquainted with the compass, the Chinese have always been as unenterprising in sailoring as in everything else, and seldom lose sight of the land, if they can help it. Their fondness for hugging the coast was very noticeable to me, and, unused to the constant vigilance and care which a long sea voyage demands, their system of duty was very lax and careless. There were no proper watches; at nightfall the Ty Kong used quietly to lower about three reefs of the main-sail and the whole of the mizzen. All the crew would then go to their cabin, leaving the helmsmen alone on deck. At midnight a supper was prepared, and the sleepers awakened. The meal ended, the helm would be relieved and the men retired to their berths again.

At this rate it may be supposed that we made slow progress, and more than one incipient mutiny had to be dealt with, some of the crew refusing to work, and the soldiers complaining on the far from unreasonable ground that they had not enough to eat. We spoke several northward-bound vessels, both native and foreign, to whom we wished to entrust the discontented warriors, but these ships one and all gratefully but firmly declined the compliment. By dint of necessity, aided by the mandarin's promises, we struggled along, and as everything must come to an end some time or other, we reached our port at the beginning of January.

I have little more to add. Ki-Chang showed himself grateful, and not only entertained me royally, but gave me substantial pecuniary aid, a thing I was in very pressing need of. Of course I have long since repaid his loan.

I obtained a passage in a French steamer to Callao, whence I made my way overland to San Francisco. I called on Mr. H——, who informed me that the *Columbia* (not then in port) had made another successful trip, but with results so diminished in the pecuniary sense that he had determined not to risk her again for inadequate profits. *Columbia*, I may say, was not the steamer's real name.

I next met Webster at Sydney. The explanation of my being left behind at Port Arthur was simple enough. The "houtcast" had taken so many "caulkers" of rum during the day that he became oblivious to the fact of my being ashore, and Chubb took it for granted that I had returned on board, especially as I had sent back the boat in which I landed with the Chinese agent. My absence was not noted until the small hours of the ensuing morning, when the swift steamer was far enough away. Webster wanted to put back for me, but Chubb, whose regards were strictly confined to number one, decided against it, coolly saying that they could pick me up next trip, and that as it was Webster's fault I had been left, he, Webster, might if he liked swim back for me. This unmessmate-like conduct, when recounted to me, so excited my ire, that if the worthy Chubb had been within kicking distance at the time, he should have known something further about it. I have not, however, seen him since.

Such were the things I saw and did where the Dragon Flag waves in splendid impotence. I took no notes of anything, excepting as to the build and fittings of the junk, and that merely for my own information, and it was not until long after that the idea of writing an account of these occurrences entered my mind; but I can trust my memory for the main events. If my little narrative should for only a few furnish not merely entertainment but admonition, I shall not have gone through quite uselessly my varied and painful experience of life.

THE END

Richard Clay & Sons, Limited, London & Bungay.